Ina Garten's 2025 Biography

The Memoir of the Woman Behind Barefoot Contessa

Carolina Bennett

CBY
PRESS

Published by
CBY Press

Ordering Information:
Quantity sales: Special discounts are available on quantity purchases by corporations, associations, and others.
For details, reach out to the publisher.

First published by CBY Press, 2025

Contents

INTRODUCTION

THE BAREFOOT CONTESSA'S JOURNEY

Ina Garten, affectionately known as the "Barefoot Contessa," has become one of the most beloved figures in the culinary world. With her signature charm, effortless style, and impeccable taste, she has inspired countless home cooks to embrace the art of simple, elegant meals. Over the past few decades, Ina's influence has extended far beyond the kitchen, transforming her from a specialty food store owner in East Hampton into a lifestyle icon whose cookbooks, television shows, and products have become household staples. But behind the poised, smiling woman in front of the camera is a story of determination, passion, and an unwavering dedication to her craft.

Born in Brooklyn and raised in Stamford, Connecticut, Ina never imagined she would become a culinary superstar. Her early life was rooted in academics and government work, a path that seemed far from the world of food. After earning her degree in economics and working in the White House as a budget analyst, Ina's career took an unexpected turn when she made a bold decision to leave her secure job and pursue her passion for cooking. This leap of faith led her to purchase a small, struggling food store in East Hampton, New York–a decision that would change her life forever.

The transformation of the Barefoot Contessa store became the foundation of her success. With no formal culinary training, Ina relied on her passion and natural instinct for good food to turn her dream into reality. She threw herself into learning every aspect of the business, from stocking shelves to cooking meals for her growing clientele. Through trial and error, she developed a keen sense of what her customers wanted–food that was both gourmet and accessible. Over time, the shop became renowned for its high-quality dishes and warm, inviting atmosphere. Ina's years at the helm of the store not only honed her cooking skills but also built her reputation as a businesswoman and culinary expert.

Ina's rise to national prominence began when she took the lessons she learned in her store and translated them into bestselling cookbooks. With the release of her first book, *The Barefoot Contessa Cookbook*, in 1999, she captured the attention of home cooks everywhere. Her recipes were straightforward, her writing warm and encouraging, and her philosophy simple: food should be both delicious and easy to make. Ina's honest acknowledgment that "cooking is hard" resonated with her readers. She didn't shy away from the challenges of preparing a meal but offered practical advice to make it easier, empowering cooks to take on even the most daunting recipes with confidence.

Her television debut in 2002 on the Food Network brought her even closer to her audience. Viewers were drawn to Ina's relaxed, no-fuss approach and her ability to create an inviting, comfortable atmosphere on screen. Unlike many celebrity chefs, she wasn't interested in using flashy techniques or intimidating ingredients. Instead, she showed how simple dishes, made with love and care, could become extraordinary. Whether she was preparing a meal for her husband Jeffrey or hosting a casual dinner party for friends, Ina's joy in cooking was contagious. Her catchphrase, "How easy is that?" became a mantra for home cooks everywhere, reminding them that great food doesn't have to be complicated.

What truly sets Ina Garten apart is her unwavering authenticity. Throughout her career, she has remained grounded, never straying from her core belief that cooking is about more than just food–it's about bringing people together and creating moments of connection. Ina's enduring success lies in her ability to make the kitchen feel like a welcoming place, even for those who find cooking daunting. Her journey from a government analyst to a culinary icon is a testament to the power of following one's passion, and her story continues to inspire fans around the world.

In this memoir, *Ina Garten: New 2024 Memoir: An Autobiography*, we will journey through the milestones of Ina's remarkable life, from her childhood to her rise to fame, and explore how she became a culinary icon. Through her own words and reflections, we'll uncover the trials, triumphs, and lessons that have shaped her career. Whether you're a longtime fan or discovering her for the first time, Ina's story will inspire you to approach life–and the kitchen–with grace, simplicity, and a dash of confidence.

CHAPTER 1

EARLY YEARS: A TASTE FOR LIFE

Family Dynamics, Parental Influence, and Sibling Bonds

Ina Garten's upbringing in Brooklyn, New York, was shaped by the values instilled by her parents, Charles and Florence Rosenberg, and the family dynamics she navigated with her older brother, Kenneth. Charles Rosenberg, a surgeon known for his professional achievements, placed a strong emphasis on independence, self-reliance, and hard work. He encouraged his children to set ambitious goals and pursue them with confidence, lessons that would later resonate with Ina as she built her career. His belief in Ina's potential became a cornerstone of her development, even as she pursued a less conventional path.

Florence Rosenberg had a different approach, prioritizing academic excellence and intellectual pursuits over creative hobbies. Florence did not encourage Ina's interest in cooking, believing it was not a productive use of time. This tension between Ina's budding love for food and her mother's preference for academic success created an undercurrent of resistance. Ina learned to explore her culinary passions independently, a dynamic that shaped her drive to follow her instincts despite societal or familial expectations. Though Florence's emphasis on discipline and structure provided Ina with essential tools for success, the lack of support for her creative side made her early culinary explorations more of a personal rebellion.

Ina's brother Kenneth, who followed a traditional path into medicine, reinforced family expectations around professional success. While their relationship was supportive, Kenneth's career choices added subtle pressure on Ina to conform to similar expectations. However, her divergence from the prescribed path of conventional success was also a testament to her determination to carve her own niche. The contrast between Kenneth's structured ambitions and Ina's creative pursuits highlighted her growing sense of independence and desire to pursue a life that reflected her passions.

Ultimately, Ina's family dynamics taught her the importance of discipline, self-confidence, and perseverance, while also instilling in her a need to explore her creative passions on her own terms. These early influences shaped her entrepreneurial mindset and prepared her to embrace challenges, eventually leading her to success in the culinary world.

Growing Up in New York: Cultural and Culinary Exposure

Ina's childhood in Brooklyn exposed her to a vibrant food culture that profoundly shaped her future cooking philosophy. The city's culinary landscape offered a wide variety of influences, from Jewish delis serving bagels and smoked fish to Italian bakeries offering fresh bread and pastries. These early experiences with artisanal foods introduced Ina to the importance of high-quality ingredients, a principle that would become central to her cooking style. Family visits to local specialty shops and markets provided sensory experiences that deepened her appreciation for fresh produce and handmade products.

Though these outings with her parents were not specifically intended to nurture her interest in cooking, they left a lasting impact. Ina absorbed the joy of browsing bustling markets, savoring the smells of fresh bread, and seeing colorful displays of fruits and vegetables. These moments awakened her love for food and sparked her curiosity about how ingredients could be transformed into meals that brought people together.

The family's move to Stamford, Connecticut, in her childhood presented a shift from the bustling, diverse environment of Brooklyn to a quieter, more suburban lifestyle. While the new setting had fewer cultural stimuli, Ina adapted by focusing more on home-based activities, including cooking. She began organizing small gatherings with friends, experimenting with food, and exploring hospitality as a way to bring joy to others. Even at a young age, she understood that food could be more than sustenance—it could foster connection and create memorable experiences.

These dual influences—urban Brooklyn's culinary vibrancy and suburban Stamford's home-based hospitality—shaped Ina's approach to food. She learned to balance sophistication with simplicity, blending the elegance of artisanal ingredients with the warmth of home cooking. These early lessons laid the foundation for the cooking philosophy she would later develop: making high-quality, delicious meals accessible and enjoyable for everyone.

Early Inspirations and Experimenting with Cooking

Despite her mother's discouragement, Ina's passion for cooking grew during her formative years. She found creative ways to explore her interest, starting with small culinary experiments like baking cookies and helping with family meals. These early experiences gave her a sense of accomplishment and hinted at the deeper joy she found in preparing food for others. Holiday gatherings, filled with traditional Jewish dishes, further demonstrated the emotional power of food, reinforcing her belief that meals could foster connection and celebration.

Ina's love for cooking blossomed during her teenage years, when she became the designated family entertainer. Organizing dinners and hosting friends provided her with opportunities to experiment with new recipes and develop her skills in hospitality. These gatherings allowed her to discover that food could not only nourish but also create moments of joy and connection–a theme that would become central to her identity as the Barefoot Contessa.

A pivotal moment in Ina's culinary journey came when she discovered Julia Child's *Mastering the Art of French Cooking*. Child's approach to French cuisine was revolutionary, presenting complex dishes in a way that felt accessible and achievable. Inspired by the book, Ina began experimenting with more ambitious recipes, gaining confidence with each success. This marked the beginning of her lifelong love for French cuisine, which would later influence many of her own recipes.

In addition to Child's influence, early cooking shows played a significant role in shaping Ina's approach to food. Programs that broke down recipes into simple steps reinforced her belief that anyone could create beautiful meals with the right guidance. These influences demystified cooking for Ina, encouraging her to embrace trial and error as part of the learning process. Over time, this approach became a defining characteristic of her cooking style: blending elegance with simplicity and always prioritizing the joy of sharing meals with loved ones.

Love and Partnership with Jeffrey Garten

Ina Garten's relationship with Jeffrey Garten has been one of the most significant influences on her personal life and career. Their love story began when Ina was a teenager. Jeffrey, who was five years her senior, saw a picture of her during a visit to Dartmouth College and sent her a letter—a bold move that sparked their lifelong relationship. They married in 1968, beginning a partnership grounded in love, trust, and unwavering mutual support. Jeffrey's progressive views on gender roles allowed Ina the freedom to explore her passions without feeling restricted by societal expectations, a rarity for the time.

When Jeffrey was stationed at Fort Bragg, North Carolina, as part of his military service, Ina used this period to dive deeper into her love for cooking. Hosting dinner parties for Jeffrey's colleagues gave her the perfect opportunity to experiment with recipes and develop her hospitality skills. These gatherings reinforced her belief that food could do more than nourish—it could create meaningful connections. The appreciation she received from guests further motivated her to pursue cooking with more seriousness, setting the stage for her eventual transition into a culinary career.

Jeffrey's support was unwavering during these formative years. He encouraged her to follow her passion, reassuring her that exploring cooking was just as valid as traditional career paths. His belief in her abilities was instrumental in helping Ina develop the confidence she needed to consider taking bold steps later in life. Even as Jeffrey pursued his career in finance and academia, their relationship thrived, with both supporting one another's ambitions. Their strong partnership has been a defining aspect of Ina's life, as evident in how often Jeffrey's presence—both physically and emotionally—has been woven into her work, from her early endeavors to her bestselling cookbooks and television shows.

Balancing Academic Pursuits with Culinary Passions

In her early years, Ina Garten's life followed a more conventional path. She enrolled at Syracuse University, majoring in economics to align with her parents' expectations. Academic excellence came naturally to her, but she found herself increasingly drawn to cooking, a passion that felt out of sync with her formal education. Ina's parents, particularly her mother Florence, valued intellectual accomplishments over creative pursuits. Consequently, she didn't receive encouragement to pursue cooking at the time, even though it brought her joy.

After her marriage to Jeffrey, their frequent moves due to his military career gave Ina an opportunity to immerse herself in cooking wherever they lived. Preparing meals and hosting small gatherings became her creative outlet amid the transitions, helping her find stability and joy. Each new location allowed Ina to experiment with different ingredients and cuisines, gradually refining her skills in the kitchen.

When Jeffrey was stationed in Washington, D.C., Ina secured a position at the White House Office of Management and Budget. Although she excelled professionally, she quickly realized that the routine of government work did not bring her personal fulfillment. Weekends became her sanctuary, offering her the chance to cook, host dinners, and entertain friends. These gatherings not only allowed her to explore her passion but also offered a glimpse into how much joy she could bring to others through food and hospitality.

Despite the dichotomy between her career and her passion, Ina's time in academia and government helped her build essential skills, such as project management and budgeting, that would later become invaluable when running her business. However, she soon realized that while she could excel in traditional roles, they didn't align with her true interests. With each passing year, the pull toward cooking grew stronger, culminating in a life-changing decision that would alter the course of her career forever.

Shifting from Government Work to Culinary Pursuits

By the late 1970s, Ina Garten found herself increasingly dissatisfied with her government career. Despite her achievements at the Office of Management and Budget, she felt that crunching numbers and managing energy policies did not align with her true passion. "I didn't want to do spreadsheets for the rest of my life," Ina later recalled. Cooking and hosting gatherings on weekends continued to provide an emotional outlet and a sense of fulfilment that her government job could not. The joy she derived from preparing meals and creating welcoming environments for friends hinted at the possibility of turning her passion into something more substantial.

Jeffrey's encouragement played a crucial role during this transitional period. He understood Ina's growing frustration with her career and reassured her that it was okay to take risks. His unwavering belief in her abilities gave Ina the confidence to explore new opportunities, despite the uncertainties. In 1978, while scanning the classifieds section of *The New York Times*, Ina stumbled upon an advertisement for a small food store for sale in Westhampton Beach, New York. The store, called Barefoot Contessa, specialized in gourmet products, and the idea of owning it immediately captured Ina's imagination.

Although Ina lacked formal culinary training or business experience, she decided to take the plunge. Jeffrey's enthusiastic support was pivotal, helping her overcome her fears and embrace the unknown. The couple took on financial risks to purchase the store, embarking on an entrepreneurial journey that would change Ina's life. Managing the Barefoot Contessa store was challenging, but Ina's dedication, combined with Jeffrey's emotional support, made it possible for her to navigate the steep learning curve.

This bold leap marked the beginning of Ina's culinary career. The transition from government analyst to food entrepreneur not only aligned with her passions but also laid the foundation for the culinary empire she would eventually build. With Jeffrey by her side, Ina discovered that following her heart–despite the risks–was the key to creating a fulfilling and successful life.

The Turning Point: Discovering the Barefoot Contessa Store

In 1978, Ina Garten's life took a transformative turn when she found an ad in *The New York Times* for a small food store for sale in Westhampton Beach, New York. Named the Barefoot Contessa, the shop specialized in gourmet foods and catered to locals and vacationers from the Hamptons. Despite having no formal culinary training or experience in retail, Ina was drawn to the idea of owning the store. Encouraged by Jeffrey, she decided to take a leap of faith, leaving behind her government career to pursue something she loved.

Running Barefoot Contessa proved challenging but invigorating. Ina handled everything from selecting high-quality ingredients to managing customer service, immersing herself fully in the business. Although the transition to entrepreneurship was demanding, her lack of formal training became a hidden advantage. Rather than following traditional culinary techniques, she focused on simple, flavorful dishes using the best possible ingredients. This down-to-earth approach made gourmet food feel accessible, attracting a loyal following.

The store became known not just for its products but also for its warm, inviting atmosphere. Ina's natural instinct for hospitality made Barefoot Contessa more than a food shop–it became a community hub. Locals and vacationers felt valued and welcomed, which differentiated the store from others in the area. Word of her expertise spread, and over the years, Ina built a reputation as a trusted culinary expert.

However, the demands of running the business became overwhelming, and by 1996, Ina decided to sell the store. Although it was a difficult decision, it allowed her to pursue new ventures, including writing cookbooks. Selling Barefoot Contessa marked the end of one chapter in her life but laid the foundation for her success as an author and television personality.

Support Networks and Family Reactions

Throughout Ina Garten's career, Jeffrey Garten was her greatest supporter. His unwavering belief in her abilities gave Ina the courage to take risks and follow her passion for food, even when the path was unconventional. At critical moments—such as buying the Barefoot Contessa store—Jeffrey's support was instrumental, assuring Ina that taking risks was worthwhile. His encouragement extended beyond words; Jeffrey actively participated in Ina's journey, providing emotional stability as she navigated the challenges of entrepreneurship.

Initially, some family members were skeptical about Ina's decision to leave a stable government career to run a food store. Given her lack of culinary training and the financial risks involved, their doubts were understandable. However, as Ina's success became evident, skepticism gave way to admiration. Watching her transform the Barefoot Contessa store into a thriving business demonstrated her capabilities, earning her the respect of family and friends alike.

Ina's support network extended beyond Jeffrey to include friends and colleagues. Their encouragement during moments of self-doubt reinforced her belief that pursuing her passion was the right choice. Ina later reflected that these relationships were invaluable, giving her the strength to embrace uncertainty and persevere through the challenges of running a business. Even in the most difficult times, knowing she had people who believed in her made all the difference.

The transition from a government analyst to a food entrepreneur was far from easy. Ina had to learn everything from business management to customer service, often through trial and error. However, she embraced the journey with determination, knowing that she was not alone. Jeffrey's support, combined with encouragement from her wider circle, allowed her to turn challenges into opportunities, ultimately laying the foundation for her future success.

Ina Garten's early life and career were shaped by family expectations, personal exploration, and the courage to follow her passion for food. From experimenting in the kitchen as a child to buying the Barefoot Contessa store, every step in her journey contributed to her growth as both a cook and a businesswoman. The support she received from Jeffrey and her wider network of friends and family was essential, giving her the confidence to embrace her love for cooking and hospitality.

Selling the Barefoot Contessa store in 1996 marked a turning point, allowing Ina to transition into new ventures, including writing cookbooks and hosting a television show. Through these opportunities, she reached an even larger audience, inspiring millions to embrace simple, delicious food. Ina's story exemplifies the power of following one's passion, even when the path forward is uncertain. Her journey is a testament to how determination, discipline, and a strong support network can turn a passion into a lifelong career.

Ina Garten's success also reflects her belief that food is about more than just sustenance–it is a way to connect with others and bring joy into everyday life. Whether hosting intimate dinner parties or managing a bustling food store, Ina discovered that food could foster meaningful connections. Her journey from government analyst to culinary icon is a reminder that it's never too late to pursue what makes you truly happy. With passion, persistence, and the right support, any dream can become a reality.

CHAPTER 2

FROM GOVERNMENT TO GOURMET

In the early years of Ina Garten's life, Washington, D.C. represented opportunity, purpose, and prestige—a place where ambition thrived and public service was a calling. For Ina, it was also the backdrop to her transition from newlywed to professional, a city that shaped her sense of self and tested her resolve. Her journey in D.C. would see her navigate the complexities of government work, balance the demands of a growing marriage, and eventually confront the tension between security and passion.

In this chapter, we explore how Ina adapted to the unique pressures of life in the nation's capital, working as a budget analyst at the White House while Jeffrey built a promising career in international affairs. D.C. was demanding, and while she took pride in her government role, the routine soon began to weigh on her. At first, she found solace in small pleasures—weekends spent cooking and entertaining friends—but over time, those moments became more than a distraction. They awakened a dormant passion, sparking dreams of a different life altogether.

Through the lens of her years in Washington, this chapter captures the transformative power of choice. It traces how Ina found herself at a crossroads between staying in a stable career and taking the leap into the unknown. With Jeffrey's steadfast support, she would soon realize that sometimes, the most difficult decisions are the ones that lead us to our truest selves.

Life in Washington, D.C.

In the early 1970s, Washington, D.C., was a city of power and purpose. The nation's capital buzzed with political energy, shaped by shifting administrations, ambitious civil servants, and a government bureaucracy that thrived on policy debates and constant negotiation. For Ina Garten, D.C. marked the beginning of a new chapter—one filled with excitement but also unexpected challenges. Moving to the city as a newlywed with her husband, Jeffrey, who was beginning a promising career in the military and finance sectors, represented both an adventure and a significant adjustment. Though brimming with optimism, Ina soon discovered that transitioning into this new life would require far more than she had anticipated.

Both Ina and Jeffrey were driven by the excitement of their budding careers. They had married young, filled with the confidence that they could build the life they dreamed of together. However, as the honeymoon phase faded, the reality of life in D.C. set in. The pace of the city was relentless–days filled with work commitments, professional obligations, and social events, all while they were still figuring out their rhythm as a couple. The transition from carefree college graduates to a professional couple in a high-powered environment was anything but smooth. D.C.'s culture demanded precision, ambition, and long hours, forcing Ina to quickly develop new routines that would help her thrive both personally and professionally.

Adjusting to a New Environment

The demands of life in Washington forced Ina to step outside her comfort zone. No longer just the girl from a small town in Connecticut, Ina was now immersed in a world where careers defined social status and achievement was paramount. The expectations placed on her were both external and internal–she felt the pressure to support Jeffrey as he juggled his military obligations and international finance ambitions while also carving out her own career. Jeffrey's work often took him away for long periods, requiring her to find balance and independence in their marriage.

Initially, the adjustment was overwhelming. Jeffrey's job placed him at the intersection of military strategy and financial planning, often requiring travel and long hours. In his absence, Ina took it upon herself to keep their home life running smoothly. Whether it meant dealing with household responsibilities or providing emotional support during Jeffrey's stressful days, Ina took pride in maintaining the foundation of their relationship. At the same time, she wanted more than just a role as a supportive wife–she was determined to build a meaningful career of her own. This juggling act–managing a household, nurturing a marriage, and navigating a career–became a defining challenge of her years in Washington.

Her own introduction to professional life added another layer of complexity. The bureaucratic world of Washington, where every conversation was a negotiation and every meeting carried weight, demanded a mindset far different from what Ina had known before. There were budgets to analyze, policies to implement, and office politics to navigate. In such a competitive environment, standing out required focus, persistence, and adaptability. But it also left little room for spontaneity, forcing Ina to be intentional about how she spent her time and energy.

Moments of Joy Amid the Hustle

Despite the demands of their professional lives, Ina and Jeffrey made it a point to find joy in the little moments they shared together. Evenings became opportunities to reconnect, carving out small but meaningful rituals that kept their bond strong. Sometimes, they would go for long walks through the National Mall, taking in the beauty of the monuments illuminated at night. On other occasions, they enjoyed quiet dinners at home, savoring meals Ina prepared while exchanging stories about their day. Coffee on the balcony, a shared bottle of wine, or a weekend picnic became their way of slowing down and savoring life amidst the constant hustle of the capital.

These moments, though seemingly small, were vital to maintaining their connection. D.C. was a city where personal ambitions often strained relationships, but Ina and Jeffrey were determined to support each other. Their love for good food became one of their favorite ways to unwind–cooking together or hosting friends gave them a shared passion that transcended the stress of their work lives. The more they entertained, the more Ina realized that these experiences brought her genuine joy. Cooking wasn't just a necessity; it was becoming a creative outlet, one that provided balance to the demanding nature of their professional routines.

Balancing Work and Marriage

For many couples of the era, traditional gender roles often meant that one partner's career took precedence over the other's. However, Ina and Jeffrey's marriage was a partnership rooted in mutual respect and shared ambition. Both were determined to succeed professionally, but neither wanted to do so at the expense of their relationship. It wasn't always easy. There were moments when Jeffrey's long hours or frequent travel created distance, leaving Ina to manage their personal life on her own. Yet, rather than resenting the challenges, Ina embraced them, determined to build a life that was fulfilling both inside and outside the home.

The key to their partnership was balance. Jeffrey's work in international affairs often took center stage, but Ina found ways to support his career without neglecting her own aspirations. When Jeffrey had to travel for work, Ina took the opportunity to focus on her own goals, using the time to hone her skills and grow more independent. In turn, Jeffrey made sure to prioritize their time together when he was home, never letting his career overshadow the importance of their relationship. Their ability to support each other's ambitions while maintaining a deep personal connection became a cornerstone of their marriage.

Weekends were particularly special for them–a time to step away from the pressures of their careers and simply enjoy each other's company. Sometimes that meant a quiet evening spent reading side by side or hosting friends for dinner parties that Ina planned with meticulous care. These gatherings became a highlight of their week, not just because they loved entertaining but because they reminded each other of the joy they found in shared experiences. With each meal Ina prepared, she felt more connected to something that fed her soul in a way government work never could.

A Foundation for the Future

Looking back, it's clear that Ina's time in Washington was pivotal–not just in terms of her career but in shaping the values and habits that would guide her in the years to come. D.C. forced her to grow in ways she hadn't expected, teaching her resilience, discipline, and the importance of balancing ambition with personal fulfillment. It was a period of growth, both as an individual and as part of a partnership. The lessons she learned during these years–how to navigate a demanding environment, maintain a strong marriage, and find joy in small moments–would become invaluable as she prepared to take the next step in her life's journey.

Though Ina hadn't yet realized it, these early experiences in Washington were laying the foundation for her future. The long hours, the dinner parties, the quiet moments with Jeffrey—they were all pieces of a larger puzzle, one that would eventually lead her to discover her true passion. For now, however, she was content to take things one day at a time, building a life that was both meaningful and full of love, all the while planting the seeds of a dream that was slowly beginning to take shape.

The Spark of a Culinary Dream

Finding Refuge in Cooking

During her years in Washington, D.C., Ina Garten found herself caught between two worlds. On one side was her demanding government career, where she spent her weekdays navigating energy policy and balancing budgets. On the other side was the quiet joy she discovered on weekends, when the weight of government work lifted, and she could return to something deeply personal: cooking. Saturday and Sunday became her sanctuary, a time when the pressures of the workweek melted away and the kitchen became her domain.

Ina's modest D.C. apartment, though far from extravagant, became the heart of these moments. It was where she began hosting small dinner parties, inviting friends and colleagues over for meals she prepared with care and creativity. Planning menus, shopping for ingredients, and trying out new recipes gave her a renewed sense of purpose. In these moments, Ina felt more like herself than she ever did sitting at a desk at the Office of Management and Budget. Each dish she created gave her a sense of satisfaction she struggled to find in her professional life, and the joy she felt watching her guests savor her food was unmatched.

Cooking became more than just a chore—it was her therapy. In the kitchen, she could control outcomes in a way that government work didn't allow. Decisions were immediate: adding a pinch of salt, adjusting the heat, or whisking until just the right consistency was achieved. The satisfaction was tangible and immediate. Unlike her job, where results were buried under layers of bureaucracy, cooking offered creative freedom and instant feedback. It gave her a sense of accomplishment and personal fulfillment that she had been yearning for. The applause of friends around the dinner table was a stark contrast to the dry reports and meetings that filled her workdays.

As Ina grew more confident in the kitchen, the dinners she hosted became more elaborate. She loved experimenting with new techniques, borrowing from French cuisine or adding her personal twist to traditional recipes. Her friends noticed. They began to comment on her growing culinary talent, frequently asking for recipes or marveling at how effortlessly she orchestrated the meals. These compliments planted a seed–one that hinted at the possibility that cooking might be more than just a hobby. With every dinner party, Ina's passion for food deepened, and she began to see the kitchen as more than a place for weekend experiments. It was becoming the place where she felt most alive.

Building Confidence through Entertaining

As Ina's dinner parties grew in frequency, so did the feedback from her guests. It wasn't just polite appreciation; it was genuine admiration. Guests were not only impressed with her food–they were enchanted by the entire experience she curated. Ina had a way of making people feel comfortable, welcome, and well-fed. It was clear that food, for her, wasn't just about nourishment. It was a way to create moments of connection and joy. With every compliment from her guests, Ina began to see herself not just as an amateur home cook but as someone with a real gift for entertaining.

Friends would often tell her, "You have a knack for this! You could do this professionally." Although she initially brushed off these remarks as mere encouragement, the idea lingered. Could she really turn her passion for cooking and entertaining into something more? Each positive comment chipped away at her self-doubt, slowly building her confidence. What started as casual dinner gatherings began to feel like previews of something larger–a life centered around food and community.

Ina loved every part of the process. From crafting menus to setting the perfect table, she found joy in the details. Her guests noticed the thoughtfulness in each meal and how every dish complemented the next. These gatherings became more than just meals; they were experiences, carefully curated with an eye for balance and comfort. Ina thrived on the challenge of making each dinner party unique, using food to set the tone and create lasting memories.

As the praise continued, the spark of an idea began to form: What if food could be more than a hobby? What if this passion–this ability to bring people together over a good meal–was her real calling? The idea excited and frightened her in equal measure. It was a dream that seemed both exhilarating and impossible, a vision of a life she wasn't yet sure she had the courage to pursue.

Dreaming of a Different Life

As Ina's love for cooking grew, her enthusiasm for her government job began to fade. Each week, she found it harder to muster the energy for her work at the Office of Management and Budget. The long hours, the endless policy discussions, and the meticulous spreadsheets no longer inspired her. Instead, they began to feel like a burden–something she endured rather than enjoyed. In contrast, cooking gave her life a sense of vibrancy and meaning that government work could never match.

As time passed, the contrast between the two worlds became starker. The government job provided stability and prestige, but it felt empty compared to the joy she found in the kitchen. She began to dream of a different life–one where she could dedicate herself fully to food and hospitality. The idea of spending her days experimenting with recipes, planning menus, and hosting guests filled her with excitement. But the thought of leaving her secure career behind was daunting. After all, she had spent years building her government career, and walking away from it felt like a tremendous risk.

Ina wrestled with doubt. What if things didn't work out? What if cooking was just a fleeting passion, not a sustainable career? The idea of starting over in an entirely new field was terrifying, especially in a city like Washington, where stability and status were highly valued. There were moments when she questioned whether it was foolish to even entertain the thought. Yet, despite her fears, the dream persisted.

The more she thought about it, the clearer it became: Staying in her government job meant denying herself the chance to explore a life she truly loved. She knew that if she continued down the path she was on, she would always wonder "what if." The thought of spending the next few decades feeling unfulfilled was far scarier than the prospect of failure. The dream of building a life around food had taken root, and it was growing stronger with each passing day.

Ina wasn't quite ready to make the leap, but the possibility was no longer just a fleeting thought. It was becoming a real consideration, one that she knew she couldn't ignore for much longer. Cooking had become more than a refuge–it had become a calling. And though the road ahead was uncertain, one thing was becoming increasingly clear: A life centered around food was the life Ina was meant to live.

Taking the Leap: Leaving D.C. for a New Life

The Moment of Decision

The turning point for Ina Garten came one quiet evening as she and Jeffrey sat together, reflecting on their future. The question of "what's next?" had been hovering over their conversations for months, but that night, it finally took center stage. Ina, her voice laden with frustration, admitted to Jeffrey that her heart was no longer in government work. She confessed that the thrill she had once felt at the Office of Management and Budget had faded. More than that, she felt disconnected from the life she was living–trapped in a role that no longer reflected who she was or what she wanted.

What surprised Ina most was Jeffrey's response. Rather than expressing concern or urging caution, Jeffrey responded with immediate and unwavering support. He had seen firsthand the joy that cooking brought Ina and believed in her ability to turn that passion into something meaningful. His confidence in her was a lifeline. With a calm certainty, Jeffrey told Ina that she should pursue what made her happy, no matter how uncertain the path might seem. Life, he reminded her, was too short to spend doing work that didn't bring joy. That conversation became the turning point. Ina knew, in that moment, that it was time to leave the security of her government job and follow her dream.

Jeffrey's Role in the Decision

Jeffrey's encouragement was a defining factor in Ina's decision to leave D.C. and pursue a different life. His belief in her was unwavering, and it gave Ina the courage she needed to embrace the unknown. Where she saw risk, Jeffrey saw opportunity. He assured her that they would figure out the transition together and that whatever challenges lay ahead, they could handle them. His faith in her talent wasn't just comforting–it was empowering.

For Ina, knowing that Jeffrey was fully behind her made all the difference. She had spent years building a stable career in public service, and the idea of leaving it all behind felt daunting. But Jeffrey's confidence in her was a steadying force, reminding her that change, while frightening, could also be liberating. With his support, Ina began to see the possibility of a new life not as an impossible dream but as an exciting challenge–one worth pursuing. Jeffrey's role wasn't just that of a supportive spouse; he became her partner in every sense, helping her chart a course toward a life built around her passions.

Overcoming Doubts and Fears

Despite Jeffrey's encouragement, Ina couldn't completely escape the doubts that crept into her mind. Leaving a secure career, especially one with the prestige of working at the White House, felt like a gamble. What if it didn't work out? What if her passion for cooking wasn't enough to build a sustainable career? And what if she regretted leaving behind the stability she had worked so hard to achieve? These questions haunted her during the weeks leading up to her decision.

Ina and Jeffrey talked through her fears, acknowledging the risks and uncertainties ahead. They knew that pursuing a new path would come with its own challenges–there were no guarantees. But they also knew that the greater risk was staying in a job that no longer fulfilled her. The thought of waking up every day, dreading the work she once cared about, was far more unsettling than the possibility of failure. As Jeffrey reminded her, failure wasn't the worst thing that could happen. What would be worse was not trying at all and spending the rest of her life wondering what might have been.

With each conversation, Ina felt a little more grounded. Jeffrey's calm, thoughtful approach helped her reframe her fears, focusing not on the obstacles but on the possibilities. The more they talked, the more Ina began to believe in the path ahead. The fears didn't disappear, but they no longer felt insurmountable. Instead, they became part of the journey–challenges to be navigated, not reasons to turn back.

Planning the Transition

Leaving D.C. required more than just emotional readiness; it demanded careful planning. Ina and Jeffrey spent months preparing for the transition, ensuring they had a solid foundation to support this new chapter in their lives. They began by reviewing their finances, calculating how much they would need to live comfortably while Ina explored new opportunities. Jeffrey's career provided some stability, but they wanted to make sure they had a financial cushion in case the transition took longer than expected.

At the same time, they started looking beyond Washington, searching for a place where Ina could fully immerse herself in her culinary passion. Moving away from D.C. was a big decision, but they knew that starting fresh in a new environment would give Ina the freedom to reinvent herself. They explored different locations, considering what each place could offer in terms of lifestyle, opportunities, and community. Every detail mattered. They weren't just planning a move; they were planning a life–one that aligned with Ina's dreams and values.

The process was both exciting and nerve-wracking. There were moments when the uncertainty felt overwhelming, but with each step they took, Ina felt a growing sense of liberation. She was no longer confined by the expectations of her government career. Instead, she was moving toward something that felt deeply authentic. The idea of building a life around her love for food wasn't just a dream anymore–it was a real possibility, one they were actively working toward.

Embracing a New Path

As the pieces began to fall into place, Ina felt a profound shift. She was no longer tethered to a life that didn't fit her; she was moving toward a life that felt aligned with who she was becoming. The fear of the unknown still lingered, but it was accompanied by a sense of excitement she hadn't felt in years. Each step toward their new life—each decision, each plan—reinforced the idea that they were on the right path.

The decision to leave D.C. wasn't just about walking away from a government job; it was about embracing the freedom to pursue what truly mattered. Ina knew that challenges lay ahead, but she also knew that she was finally living in alignment with her passions. With Jeffrey by her side, she felt ready to face whatever came next.

The night they finalized their decision, Ina and Jeffrey opened a bottle of wine to celebrate—not just the decision itself but the life they were building together. It was a moment of quiet joy and anticipation, the beginning of a new chapter filled with possibility. Ina had taken the leap, and for the first time in a long time, she felt like she was exactly where she was meant to be.

Leaving behind the familiar comforts of Washington, D.C., was not easy, but it was necessary. Ina was no longer content to live a life that didn't align with her passions. The leap into the unknown was daunting, but it was also exhilarating. With Jeffrey's unwavering support, Ina was ready to embrace a new path—one built around food, community, and the joy of following her heart. And though the road ahead was uncertain, she knew that she was finally moving toward a life she could call her own.

CHAPTER 3

BAREFOOT BEGINNINGS: THE EAST HAMPTON DREAM

After years in the fast-paced and high-pressure world of government work in Washington, D.C., Ina Garten began to feel the weight of dissatisfaction creeping in. Despite the security and prestige of her job, she knew something essential was missing. The long hours and rigid structure of public service left little room for the joy she found in food and entertaining, passions that had become an increasingly important part of her life. As she hosted friends in her small apartment and experimented with recipes, Ina began to imagine a life that felt more in tune with her heart–a life built around creativity, community, and the simple pleasures of cooking. But dreams of change were accompanied by fear and uncertainty. Could she leave behind the stability she had worked so hard to build? Was it possible to turn her love of food into something more?

The search for a new life brought Ina and Jeffrey to East Hampton, a picturesque coastal town that offered the peace and inspiration they had longed for. It was during one of these exploratory visits that Ina stumbled upon the Barefoot Contessa specialty food store, a charming establishment that seemed to embody everything she dreamed of. With its warm atmosphere, curated products, and sense of community, the store captivated Ina, sparking both excitement and trepidation. Buying the store would mean stepping into the unknown–trading spreadsheets and policy meetings for ovens and customer orders. But it also represented the opportunity to build something deeply meaningful.

With Jeffrey's unwavering support, Ina made the bold decision to buy the store and embark on an entirely new career path. This chapter explores the moments leading up to that leap of faith, when Ina chose to leave behind the familiar comfort of her government job to follow her dream. It wasn't an easy transition. Running a food business would require more than just passion–it demanded learning the ropes of entrepreneurship, understanding customers, and developing the skills necessary to manage staff, inventory, and operations.

From the moment she took ownership, Ina discovered that turning a dream into reality came with challenges she hadn't anticipated. Yet, with each misstep, she found her footing. Ina's journey at Barefoot Contessa wasn't just about mastering the technical aspects of running a business; it was also about creating a space where food could bring people together. She quickly realized that what made her store special wasn't just the high-quality products she sold but the relationships she nurtured with her customers and community.

Barefoot Contessa became more than just a specialty food store–it became a culinary haven, a place that reflected Ina's love for simple, delicious food and meaningful connections. The lessons she learned in the store's kitchen–about the art of simplicity, the value of community, and the importance of balance–would go on to shape the rest of her career. The Barefoot Contessa store wasn't just the start of a business; it was the beginning of a new life for Ina, one rooted in joy, hospitality, and the courage to follow her heart.

Finding Barefoot Contessa: A Serendipitous Discovery

The Search for a New Life

By the mid-1970s, Ina and Jeffrey Garten found themselves yearning for a lifestyle change. Life in Washington, D.C., with its high-pressure government jobs and relentless schedules, was wearing on them. Though Jeffrey thrived in his career, and Ina had found success at the Office of Management and Budget, their fast-paced lives left little room for the simple joys they both cherished–good food, meaningful conversations, and a sense of peace. It became clear that they needed to move away from the demands of D.C. and embrace a slower, more intentional way of living.

East Hampton, a coastal retreat on Long Island, soon caught their attention. Known for its picturesque beaches, small-town charm, and artistic vibe, the town offered exactly what Ina and Jeffrey were looking for: a place where they could relax, build new routines, and live more authentically. The idea of leaving behind government work in favor of a quieter, simpler existence became more enticing with each passing day. Though the thought of moving was daunting, they knew they needed a fresh start.

Stumbling Upon the Store

It was during one of these exploratory trips to East Hampton that Ina first encountered the Barefoot Contessa specialty food store. The moment was serendipitous. Strolling through the village streets, Ina noticed the storefront—a small but charming shop with a name that immediately intrigued her. Inside, she discovered a carefully curated selection of specialty foods, wines, baked goods, and gourmet ingredients, all housed in a cozy and welcoming space. There was an energy about the store, a sense that food here was more than just sustenance—it was a way of life.

Ina was captivated. The store seemed to embody everything she loved about cooking and entertaining: high-quality ingredients, creativity, and community. The idea of running a business like Barefoot Contessa began to spark something deep within her—a desire to turn her passion for food into something tangible. As fate would have it, Ina soon learned that the store was for sale, and the possibility of buying it felt both thrilling and terrifying.

The Decision to Buy

Making the leap from government analyst to specialty food store owner was not a decision Ina took lightly. Owning a business was far outside her comfort zone, and she had no formal training in entrepreneurship or retail. She knew it would be a risky endeavor—buying a store meant financial uncertainty and leaving behind the secure career she had worked hard to build. But the more Ina thought about it, the more the idea excited her. She could imagine herself in the store, designing menus, sourcing unique ingredients, and creating a space where food lovers could gather.

Ina knew the risks, but the idea of turning her passion into a career was too compelling to ignore. The thought of staying in D.C., stuck in a job that no longer fulfilled her, became far scarier than the unknown.

Jeffrey's Support

As always, Jeffrey's unwavering support was instrumental in Ina's decision. When she hesitated, voicing her fears about the risks involved, Jeffrey reminded her that life was too short to spend it doing work that didn't bring joy. He believed in her talent and reassured her that, no matter what happened, they would navigate the challenges together. His encouragement gave Ina the confidence to follow her heart.

Together, they decided to take the plunge. Buying the Barefoot Contessa store wasn't just a business decision—it was a leap of faith, a step toward a life they both dreamed of. With excitement, fear, and hope, Ina and Jeffrey left behind the life they knew and embarked on a new adventure that would change their lives forever.

Building a Culinary Haven: Learning the Business of Food

The First Days of Ownership

Ina's first days as the owner of Barefoot Contessa were a mix of exhilaration and exhaustion. Although she had imagined the excitement of owning a food business, the reality hit her quickly—there was far more involved than cooking. Beyond selecting ingredients and creating dishes, Ina found herself plunged into the logistics of running a store. Managing inventory, meeting with suppliers, and ensuring that orders were placed on time became daily tasks. Every decision, from which products to stock to how much to order, had consequences, and she quickly realized how much she still needed to learn.

Her days were filled with challenges she had never encountered before. Suddenly, she had to understand profit margins, price points, and vendor relationships, none of which were part of her experience as a home cook or government analyst. Balancing these responsibilities felt overwhelming at times, but Ina remained determined to figure it all out. The thrill of owning something she loved kept her going, even when the learning curve felt steep. With every small victory—like successfully coordinating a supplier order or restocking a customer favorite–Ina grew more confident.

From Passion to Profession

Ina soon discovered that having a passion for food was only the beginning. Cooking for friends at home was one thing; managing a store filled with paying customers was something entirely different. She quickly realized that success required more than enthusiasm. She had to develop efficient systems to keep the store running smoothly–inventory needed to be tracked, schedules organized, and menus planned to minimize waste and maximize profits. It wasn't enough to love cooking; she had to become an effective businesswoman.

There were moments when the transition from hobby cook to business owner felt daunting. Ina made mistakes along the way–ordering too much of a certain product or misjudging how popular a dish would be. But with each setback, she learned valuable lessons. Slowly, she built routines and processes that allowed the business to grow. As she gained experience, Ina discovered a new kind of satisfaction–seeing her store flourish because of the systems she had put in place. Each day brought new challenges, but they also brought new opportunities to improve and grow.

Understanding Customers

One of the most important lessons Ina learned early on was the need to understand her customers. The store catered to both year-round locals and weekend visitors from the city, and each group had different tastes and expectations. Ina realized that building a loyal customer base required more than just offering good food–it meant paying close attention to what people wanted and being flexible enough to adjust her offerings accordingly.

Ina began experimenting with different products and menu items, carefully observing which ones resonated with her customers. Some dishes became instant favorites, while others didn't quite hit the mark. Instead of being discouraged, Ina used customer feedback to refine her offerings. Over time, she developed a deep understanding of her clientele, ensuring that Barefoot Contessa became a place people looked forward to visiting.

Staffing and Operations Challenges

Managing a team of employees was another unexpected challenge. Ina knew that finding the right staff was essential to creating the atmosphere she wanted, but hiring and training employees took time and patience. Some hires worked out beautifully, while others did not, forcing Ina to make tough decisions to maintain the store's standards.

Once she had a team in place, Ina had to learn how to manage them effectively. Coordinating schedules, assigning responsibilities, and ensuring that everyone worked together smoothly was no easy task. On top of that, she had to oversee the store's daily operations, from keeping shelves stocked to ensuring customer orders were fulfilled promptly. Balancing these tasks with the creative aspects of the business was exhausting, but Ina approached it all with determination and grace. She knew that every challenge she overcame brought her closer to building the store she had envisioned.

Creating a Welcoming Atmosphere

From the moment she opened her doors, Ina understood that Barefoot Contessa needed to be more than just a place to buy food–it had to feel like a second home. She wanted customers to feel comfortable, welcomed, and cared for every time they stepped inside. For Ina, hospitality wasn't just about offering great products; it was about creating a space where people felt truly seen.

Ina made it a point to greet customers personally, learning their names and remembering their favorite products. If someone needed cooking advice, she was always happy to offer suggestions or share recipes. These small but meaningful gestures became a hallmark of the store, setting it apart from other specialty shops. People didn't just come to Barefoot Contessa for the food–they came for the experience of being part of something special.

Creating this atmosphere took effort, but it was one of Ina's greatest joys. She believed that food was about more than just sustenance; it was a way to connect with people and create lasting memories. By focusing on hospitality, she turned Barefoot Contessa into a place where customers felt more like friends and neighbors than shoppers.

This personal touch became one of the store's defining features, laying the foundation for the brand Ina would go on to build.

With each passing day, Barefoot Contessa evolved from a small specialty food store into a thriving culinary haven. And although the journey was challenging, Ina found fulfillment in every part of it—building a business, fostering community, and sharing her love of food with everyone who walked through her doors.

Creating Community Through Food: Building Relationships with Customers

Local Connections

Ina Garten understood from the beginning that Barefoot Contessa needed to be more than just a store. To thrive, it had to become a meaningful part of the East Hampton community. Ina approached this not as a marketing strategy but as a genuine effort to connect with the people around her. She took time to engage with customers on a personal level, learning their names, listening to their preferences, and understanding the rhythms of their lives. Whether it was a local family looking for picnic supplies or weekend visitors from the city seeking gourmet treats, Ina made sure she knew what each customer valued most.

This personal approach quickly built trust and loyalty. Regular customers began to feel like friends, and word spread that Barefoot Contessa was not just a place to buy food—it was a place where people felt known and welcomed. Locals appreciated that Ina took their tastes seriously, and this relationship between store and community became one of the cornerstones of her business.

Curating the Perfect Inventory

Ina curated the store's inventory with the same care she applied to her cooking. Every product she chose was something she genuinely loved and believed her customers would enjoy. This thoughtful selection process gave Barefoot Contessa its unique character—each shelf held a blend of artisanal cheeses, fresh-baked pastries, gourmet pantry staples, and unique finds that couldn't easily be found elsewhere.

Ina understood that curating the right products meant striking a balance. She offered luxurious treats, but she also stocked high-quality everyday items that aligned with the tastes of her community. Whether it was a rustic loaf of bread or a rare bottle of olive oil, each product told a story, reflecting Ina's passion for quality. Her goal was to create an environment where customers could discover something new and exciting with every visit, making the store feel like a treasure trove for food lovers.

Signature Dishes and Products

Some of the offerings at Barefoot Contessa quickly became iconic. Ina's prepared foods–such as her famous chicken salad, roasted vegetables, and decadent desserts–were instant hits. Customers returned again and again for these favorites, often planning their meals around what was available at the store. Ina's philosophy of simple, flavorful cooking resonated with both locals and weekend visitors, who appreciated the combination of elegance and comfort in her dishes.

These signature items became part of the store's identity, creating a sense of familiarity and reliability for customers. Ina's focus on using fresh, high-quality ingredients ensured that every product met her high standards. Over time, these dishes not only became beloved staples but also embodied the values of Barefoot Contessa: simplicity, taste, and care.

Personal Touches

What truly set Barefoot Contessa apart was Ina's personal involvement in the day-to-day operations. She wasn't just a business owner–she was an active participant in her customers' experience. Ina remembered regulars' favorite orders, offered cooking tips, and even helped customers plan meals for special occasions. These small but meaningful gestures created an atmosphere of warmth and hospitality, making every visit to the store feel like a personal experience.

Ina's genuine interest in her customers' lives turned many transactions into friendships. People felt seen and appreciated, which made them eager to return. This personal touch distinguished Barefoot Contessa from other specialty stores, reinforcing the idea that food wasn't just about sustenance–it was a way to connect and build relationships.

Events and Community Engagement

Ina didn't stop at creating a welcoming store; she also found ways to engage with the community beyond the store's walls. She hosted tastings, cooking demonstrations, and special events, transforming Barefoot Contessa into a gathering place for food lovers. These events allowed customers to sample new products, learn cooking techniques, and connect with one another. For Ina, these gatherings were about more than just selling food–they were about celebrating it.

Through these events, Barefoot Contessa became a beloved community institution. Whether it was a weekend wine tasting or a casual gathering to sample pastries, these moments fostered a sense of belonging among customers. The store became a place where people came not just to shop but to share experiences and celebrate their love of good food.

Building a Legacy of Connection

Ina's efforts to build meaningful relationships with her customers laid the foundation for the future success of Barefoot Contessa and her larger brand. Through personal connections, curated products, and thoughtful engagement, Ina showed that food was about more than just nourishment–it was about hospitality, connection, and joy. The values she cultivated at Barefoot Contessa would carry through to her later work as a cookbook author and television personality, reinforcing the importance of simplicity, quality, and genuine connection in every aspect of her career.

By creating a space where people felt welcome, understood, and appreciated, Ina Garten transformed Barefoot Contessa into more than just a food store. It became a community hub, a place where relationships were formed over shared meals and good conversation. This sense of connection became the heart of Ina's philosophy, demonstrating that food, at its best, has the power to bring people together in meaningful ways.

Lessons from the Kitchen: Skills That Shaped Her Future Success

Trial and Error

The early days of running Barefoot Contessa were filled with trial and error. Though Ina Garten had a passion for food, learning the intricacies of operating a business required time and patience. She made mistakes, such as ordering too much inventory or preparing dishes that didn't resonate with customers. At times, she overestimated how much product would sell, leaving her with excess stock, or created elaborate dishes that didn't match the preferences of her clientele. But Ina never viewed these challenges as failures. Instead, she treated them as opportunities to learn.

Through each misstep, she developed a sharper sense of what worked and what didn't. For instance, she learned to streamline her offerings and focus on what customers consistently loved–simple, fresh, and delicious foods. These early lessons not only improved the store's operations but also helped Ina grow more confident in her business instincts and cooking philosophy.

The Art of Simplicity

One of the most important lessons Ina learned was the value of simplicity. While experimenting with prepared foods at the store, she discovered that customers gravitated toward dishes that were straightforward but flavorful. This realization became a guiding principle: good food didn't need to be complicated. Ina found joy in perfecting classic dishes–like roasted vegetables or chicken salad–by using high-quality ingredients and focusing on balance and flavor.

This philosophy of simplicity became a cornerstone of her cooking style. It wasn't about showing off with complex techniques but about creating food that felt accessible and satisfying. This emphasis on simplicity made her offerings appealing to a wide range of customers and would later become the defining feature of her cookbooks and television show.

Recipe Development

The Barefoot Contessa store also served as a testing ground for many of the recipes that would later appear in Ina's cookbooks and on her TV show. She experimented with different combinations, paying close attention to what customers loved. If a dish sold out quickly, Ina knew she had a winner. Over time, she built a repertoire of tried-and-true recipes that were as popular with her customers as they would be with her future readers and viewers.

The store's kitchen became Ina's laboratory, a place where she could refine her techniques and gather feedback directly from customers. Each new recipe she developed not only helped grow her business but also laid the groundwork for her future career in publishing and television.

Managing Stress and Finding Balance

Running a business came with a heavy workload, and Ina had to learn how to manage stress and maintain balance. The long hours and constant responsibilities were exhausting, especially in the early years. But Ina understood that to succeed, she needed to find time to recharge. She made a conscious effort to set boundaries and prioritize time with Jeffrey, ensuring that their personal life didn't get lost in the demands of the business.

This balance between work and well-being became essential. It taught Ina the importance of taking care of herself–an insight that would carry through to her future ventures.

Learning to Let Go

After nearly two decades of running the Barefoot Contessa store, Ina knew it was time to move on. The store had become a beloved community institution, but she felt ready for a new challenge. Selling the business was not easy–it had been such an integral part of her life. But Ina understood that personal growth often required letting go. The lessons she learned from running the store would shape the next chapter of her career, helping her transition into a new role as an author and TV personality.

This moment of letting go taught Ina that sometimes the greatest success comes from knowing when to move forward.

The Legacy of Barefoot Contessa: Laying the Foundation for Future Success

The Impact on Ina's Brand

The years Ina spent at Barefoot Contessa laid the foundation for everything that followed. The experiences she gained—developing recipes, managing a business, and building relationships—shaped her approach to food and hospitality. The values she cultivated at the store—simplicity, quality, and community—became the guiding principles of her brand. Whether in her cookbooks, TV shows, or public appearances, Ina remained committed to making cooking approachable and joyful.

Her time at Barefoot Contessa also reinforced her belief in the importance of hospitality. She had learned that food was not just about ingredients; it was about creating experiences that made people feel cared for. This philosophy became a hallmark of her brand, resonating with audiences around the world.

Customer Loyalty and Word of Mouth

The relationships Ina built at Barefoot Contessa were instrumental in her early success. Many of the customers who had shopped at the store became lifelong supporters, spreading the word about her work. When Ina began writing cookbooks and appearing on television, she already had a built-in network of fans eager to see what she would do next.

Word of mouth was crucial in building her brand. The trust she had earned through personal interactions with customers translated into trust in her cookbooks and recipes. People knew that if Ina recommended something, it would be reliable, delicious, and thoughtfully prepared.

A Lasting Inspiration

Although the store was no longer hers, the spirit of Barefoot Contessa continued to inspire Ina's work. Many of the dishes she featured in her cookbooks and television show had their origins in the store's kitchen. The lessons she learned–about simplicity, quality, and the joy of sharing food–remained central to everything she did.

The essence of Barefoot Contessa lived on in her cookbooks, which encouraged home cooks to embrace the pleasure of preparing simple, elegant meals. Her television show, with its warm, welcoming tone, reflected the same sense of hospitality that had made the store so special.

The Emotional Goodbye

Selling Barefoot Contessa was an emotional experience for Ina. The store had been her introduction to the food world, the place where she discovered her passion and built a new career. Letting go was bittersweet, but Ina knew it was the right decision. It was time to take the lessons she had learned and apply them in new ways.

Looking back, Ina reflected on the importance of taking risks and following her passion. Leaving behind a secure career in Washington, D.C., to buy a food store had been a bold move, but it had also been the most rewarding decision of her life. The success of Barefoot Contessa showed her that following her heart–and trusting herself–was the key to building a meaningful career.

The store may have been just the beginning, but it set the stage for everything that came after. From cookbooks to television, Ina's journey always led back to the same core values she had nurtured at Barefoot Contessa: hospitality, quality, and the joy of food shared with others.

CHAPTER 4

CREATING THE INA GARTEN BRAND

After nearly two decades of running the Barefoot Contessa store, Ina Garten was ready for a new challenge. Selling the store was not just an emotional goodbye–it was the start of a new chapter in her life. Though uncertain about what came next, Ina knew she wanted to continue sharing her passion for food. What began as a small idea–writing a cookbook to capture the spirit of her store–soon blossomed into something far greater. That first cookbook became a bestseller, launching Ina into a new world of opportunities and transforming her from a local food entrepreneur into a national culinary icon.

In this chapter, we explore how Ina transitioned from store owner to cookbook author and television personality, building a brand that would come to embody elegance, simplicity, and authenticity. Ina's ability to craft recipes that were both sophisticated and accessible helped her connect with home cooks everywhere, proving that delicious meals don't need to be complicated. Along the way, she cultivated meaningful relationships with other chefs, food writers, and culinary influencers, creating a strong network that amplified her reach and reputation.

Through cookbooks, television shows, and public appearances, Ina developed a unique brand rooted in her personal philosophy: use high-quality ingredients, cook with love, and keep things simple. Whether writing a recipe, filming an episode of *Barefoot Contessa*, or mentoring others, Ina's approach remained consistent. This chapter traces her journey from cookbook author to TV personality and explores how her focus on hospitality, authenticity, and joy became the heart of the Ina Garten brand–a brand that continues to inspire home cooks and food lovers around the world.

From Storefront to Cookbook: The Leap into Publishing

When Ina Garten sold the Barefoot Contessa store, she found herself at a pivotal moment. Although she knew that moving on was the right choice, it left her feeling uncertain about the next chapter of her life. Having built her identity as a store owner and entrepreneur, Ina was unsure how to channel her passion for food into something new. She longed to continue sharing the joy she found in cooking and entertaining but struggled to determine what shape that new path would take. During this period of reflection, Jeffrey offered a suggestion that initially seemed far-fetched: he encouraged her to write a cookbook.

At first, Ina dismissed the idea. The thought of writing a book felt overwhelming, and she questioned whether she had the necessary skills to pull it off. Would anyone want to read her recipes? Could she successfully transition from business owner to author? Though she had built a thriving food business, the world of publishing was unfamiliar territory. Despite her doubts, the idea stayed with her, gently taking root. Ina's desire to share the essence of Barefoot Contessa–good food, made simply and with love–gradually outweighed her fears.

With Jeffrey's unwavering encouragement, Ina began seriously considering the possibility of writing her first cookbook. She decided the book would focus on the crowd-pleasing recipes her customers loved most. By featuring familiar dishes like roast chicken, hearty salads, and decadent desserts, Ina ensured the cookbook would reflect the same approachable elegance that had made the store so popular. The goal was to create recipes that anyone could make at home, capturing the relaxed, welcoming spirit of Barefoot Contessa.

The process of writing the book was both challenging and rewarding. Ina had to learn not only how to write clear and concise recipes but also how to convey her cooking philosophy–simple yet refined food that brought joy to both the cook and the guests. She focused on dishes she knew well, those that embodied her belief that cooking should be an enjoyable experience, not a stressful one. Alongside practical tips and personal anecdotes, the book aimed to inspire confidence in home cooks, encouraging them to embrace both creativity and simplicity in the kitchen.

In 1999, *The Barefoot Contessa Cookbook* was published, and to Ina's surprise, it became an instant bestseller. Readers were drawn to the book's straightforward instructions, beautiful photography, and warm, inviting tone, which made them feel as if Ina were right there in the kitchen with them. The book's success exceeded everyone's expectations, including Ina's. It not only redefined her career but also opened doors to new opportunities she hadn't imagined, including media appearances and, eventually, her own television show.

The success of *The Barefoot Contessa Cookbook* marked the beginning of an extraordinary new chapter for Ina. What had started as a tentative leap into publishing became the foundation for a thriving career as a cookbook author and television personality. More than just a book, the project helped Ina discover a new way to share her passion for food with the world, setting the stage for everything that was to come.

Defining the Brand: Simple, Elegant, and Approachable

From the beginning, Ina Garten knew that the qualities that made Barefoot Contessa special–simplicity, elegance, and warmth–needed to be reflected in her evolving brand. Whether through cookbooks, television, or public appearances, she honed a signature style that embraced the belief that cooking should be both accessible and enjoyable. For Ina, food was not just about nourishment; it was about creating experiences that brought people together. Her recipes were crafted to strike a balance–sophisticated enough for entertaining, yet simple enough to fit seamlessly into everyday life.

A guiding principle of Ina's approach was the importance of quality. She emphasized that good cooking starts with good ingredients. Whether it was the perfect heirloom tomato, a fresh baguette, or fragrant herbs from the garden, Ina believed that high-quality, seasonal ingredients elevated even the simplest dishes. Her recipes didn't rely on complicated techniques or long ingredient lists; instead, they focused on a few core elements, allowing the natural flavors to shine. For Ina, good food wasn't about showing off–it was about celebrating the beauty of simplicity and bringing joy to those around the table.

While elegance was central to her brand, Ina worked hard to make sure her recipes remained approachable for home cooks of all skill levels. She was intentional about avoiding overly complicated techniques that might intimidate her audience. Instead, her recipes were accompanied by clear, concise instructions, peppered with practical tips and tricks she had learned over the years. Whether her readers were preparing roast chicken, pasta, or chocolate cake, they felt encouraged to experiment in the kitchen without fear of failure. Ina wanted cooking to feel like a pleasure, not a chore—a belief that resonated deeply with her growing audience.

Visual presentation also played a critical role in defining the Ina Garten brand. Each of her cookbooks was carefully designed with clean, uncluttered layouts and vibrant photography that showcased the food in all its beauty. The images were not just about aesthetics—they reinforced Ina's belief that food should be beautiful but never fussy. Her writing was warm, conversational, and filled with personal anecdotes, making readers feel as though Ina was speaking directly to them. This friendly, down-to-earth tone became one of the most beloved aspects of her work.

Ina's consistency across different platforms further cemented her brand's identity. Whether in a cookbook, on television, or in an interview, she remained true to her values of simplicity, quality, and hospitality. She built a reputation for making elegance feel achievable, and her audience connected with her authenticity. Ina's philosophy—that good food brings joy, whether for a dinner party or a weeknight meal—became the heart of her brand. Through her books, shows, and public appearances, she showed the world that anyone could create beautiful meals with minimal stress, turning cooking into a joyful experience to be shared.

Building a Network of Culinary Influencers and Friends

Ina Garten's rise to culinary stardom was not achieved in isolation. Throughout her journey, she cultivated meaningful relationships with influential figures in the food industry who provided guidance, support, and opportunities at critical points in her career. Early on, Ina connected with prominent personalities like Martha Stewart, whose philosophy of simple yet elegant living aligned perfectly with her own. Martha, a pioneer in the lifestyle industry, became a valuable mentor and friend, offering advice on navigating the publishing world and connecting Ina with a broader audience. These early relationships were instrumental in helping Ina transition smoothly from a store owner to a public figure.

Ina found that building genuine connections within the culinary world gave her not only access to resources and expertise but also credibility. Trust was an essential ingredient in her brand's success, and she earned it by forging authentic relationships with chefs, food writers, and media personalities. Many of these individuals helped promote her first cookbook, lending it early momentum through recommendations and endorsements. Appearances on popular television programs and interviews in major lifestyle magazines provided additional exposure, helping Ina reach new audiences. These opportunities were the result of both her culinary talents and her ability to cultivate strong, supportive relationships with key figures in the industry.

Ina's collaborative spirit extended beyond external connections. She was deliberate in assembling a team of talented professionals to help bring her vision to life. Editors, photographers, and assistants became critical partners in her projects, sharing her commitment to quality and consistency. Ina's attention to detail ensured that every cookbook, television episode, and media appearance reflected the same high standards she had maintained at her store. More than just coworkers, her collaborators became an integral part of her journey, and Ina treated them with the same warmth and respect she extended to her customers. This nurturing environment fostered creativity and ensured that her brand retained its authenticity across all platforms.

In addition to benefiting from her network, Ina became a mentor and source of inspiration for aspiring chefs and food professionals. Known for her generosity and kindness, she offered advice and encouragement to those starting out in the culinary field. Ina's willingness to share her experiences and insights helped her build a positive reputation within the industry, further reinforcing her role as both a talented chef and a respected mentor. Her support of others was not just about professional connections–it reflected her belief in the power of collaboration and community.

Through these relationships and partnerships, Ina established a strong foundation for her brand. Her network of culinary influencers, trusted collaborators, and mentees became instrumental in building and sustaining her success. By cultivating trust, collaboration, and authenticity, Ina was able to grow beyond her initial achievements and lay the groundwork for a career that would flourish for decades. Her story demonstrates the value of relationships in both personal and professional life, showing that success is not only about talent but also about fostering connections that inspire and uplift.

The Power of Simple, Elegant Meals: The Philosophy Behind Her Brand

At the heart of Ina Garten's brand is her belief that food is more than just nourishment–it is an expression of love and care. This philosophy permeates her cookbooks, television show, and public appearances. Ina often emphasizes that cooking for loved ones is one of the most meaningful ways to connect and show affection. Whether preparing an elaborate dinner or a simple breakfast, Ina's approach encourages people to embrace the joy of feeding others, knowing that food brings people together. Her cookbooks often feature personal anecdotes, reinforcing the idea that each dish carries an emotional element–a memory or moment worth savoring.

Simplicity has always been Ina's strength. She champions the idea that great food doesn't need to be complicated to be elegant. Her recipes often focus on a handful of high-quality ingredients, allowing their natural flavors to shine. Rather than relying on advanced techniques or exotic components, Ina's approach celebrates fresh herbs, ripe produce, and pantry staples. For her, cooking should be an enjoyable experience, not a stressful one. This simplicity has become her signature, showing home cooks that even the most sophisticated dishes can be easy to prepare. A well-cooked roast chicken or perfectly dressed salad can be just as memorable as a complex gourmet meal.

Ina also strikes a thoughtful balance between indulgence and wholesome eating. She encourages her audience to embrace indulgent treats–whether it's a rich chocolate cake or buttery pasta–without guilt. At the same time, her recipes incorporate fresh vegetables, lean proteins, and simple salads, offering options for everyday meals that are both satisfying and healthy. For Ina, food is about enjoyment and balance, and her philosophy reflects an approach to cooking and eating that celebrates pleasure without excess.

Inspiring confidence in home cooks is another key aspect of Ina's philosophy. She believes that cooking should be a rewarding, stress-free experience, and she works hard to demystify the process for her audience. Her clear instructions, practical tips, and encouraging tone empower even novice cooks to try new things. Ina often reminds her readers and viewers that perfection isn't the goal; instead, cooking is about having fun, experimenting, and creating something enjoyable. This supportive approach has made her a trusted voice for countless home cooks, many of whom feel that she is personally guiding them through each recipe. Through this philosophy, Ina has built a brand that resonates with people around the world, showing that food made with love, simplicity, and joy can make any meal special.

Expanding into Television: Bringing Her Brand to a New Audience

Ina Garten's transition from cookbook author to television personality came somewhat unexpectedly. After her early cookbooks became bestsellers, the Food Network approached Ina with the idea of developing her own cooking show. Initially, she was reluctant. The idea of being on camera felt intimidating, and she wasn't sure if she could translate her passion for food into a television format. Unlike many celebrity chefs, Ina didn't seek out the spotlight, and the thought of hosting a show seemed far outside her comfort zone. However, with gentle encouragement from her team, friends, and the network, she eventually decided to take the leap. In 2002, *Barefoot Contessa* premiered, marking the start of an exciting new chapter in her career.

Developing a natural on-screen presence took some time, but Ina quickly found her stride. Her initial nerves faded as she realized that authenticity was the key to success. Rather than trying to fit into a television persona, she embraced being herself–warm, welcoming, and relaxed. This genuine approach resonated deeply with viewers, who appreciated the sense of ease and comfort she brought to each episode. Ina's goal was not just to teach recipes but to create an atmosphere where viewers felt like they were cooking alongside a friend. Her friendly demeanor, combined with her clear instructions and practical tips, made the show feel approachable and inviting.

Television gave Ina a powerful platform to connect with a broader audience. *Barefoot Contessa* allowed her to share more than just recipes; it gave viewers glimpses of her personal life, including her relationship with Jeffrey, their charming Hamptons home, and her entertaining tips. These personal touches added depth to the show, making it feel intimate and authentic. Viewers became captivated not just by Ina's food, but by her way of living–effortlessly elegant yet grounded in simplicity and joy.

Over the years, *Barefoot Contessa* evolved while staying true to its core charm. Ina's signature style–sophisticated but easy-to-make meals–remained the heart of the show, but she also adapted to changing trends and viewer interests. From showcasing holiday feasts to preparing cozy weeknight dinners, every episode reflected Ina's philosophy that food should bring joy to everyday life. Whether she was hosting friends, preparing a romantic meal for Jeffrey, or offering advice on effortless entertaining, Ina's warmth and consistency kept viewers coming back for more.

The success of *Barefoot Contessa* solidified Ina's place as a beloved figure in the culinary world. The show's ability to adapt without losing its essence allowed it to remain a staple on the Food Network for many years. Through television, Ina reached a new audience, inspiring countless home cooks to embrace her philosophy of simple, joyful meals. With every episode, Ina proved that good food and good living could be accessible to everyone, cementing her legacy as one of the most trusted and admired figures in modern food television.

CHAPTER 5

ON TELEVISION: A NEW PLATFORM FOR SHARING

After the success of her first few cookbooks, Ina Garten was offered a surprising opportunity that would change the course of her career: a television show on the Food Network. While the idea seemed like a natural next step to many, Ina was initially reluctant. She had built a quiet, fulfilling life in the Hamptons, far removed from the spotlight. The thought of being on camera felt intimidating, and she wasn't sure if she could translate her passion for cooking and entertaining into a television format. However, with encouragement from Jeffrey and close friends, Ina decided to take the leap into television, and *Barefoot Contessa* premiered in 2002.

The transition from cookbook author to TV personality came with challenges, but Ina's warmth, authenticity, and approachable style quickly made her a natural fit for the screen. Unlike other cooking shows that focused on technical skills, *Barefoot Contessa* offered something more intimate. Filmed in Ina's own kitchen, the show welcomed viewers into her world, where cooking was about more than just following recipes–it was about creating joyful experiences for friends and family.

Ina's focus on simple, elegant meals resonated with a wide audience. Her friendly, reassuring demeanor made viewers feel capable of recreating even sophisticated dishes at home. The show also allowed Ina to share glimpses of her personal life, including her relationship with Jeffrey, which endeared her even more to her growing fanbase.

As her popularity grew, Ina remained committed to maintaining a balance between her public career and personal life. She carefully managed her time in the spotlight, setting boundaries to protect her privacy and well-being. *Barefoot Contessa* not only expanded her reach but also solidified her place as one of the most beloved figures in food television, inspiring generations of home cooks with her simple philosophy: cook with love, entertain with joy, and savor life's small moments.

The Unexpected Food Network Offer: A Reluctant Leap into Television

The opportunity to transition from bestselling author to television host came unexpectedly for Ina Garten. After the overwhelming success of her first few cookbooks, the Food Network approached her with an offer to create a cooking show. While it seemed like a natural progression to many, Ina had reservations. Public life was not something she had ever actively pursued, and she preferred the quiet, grounded lifestyle she had built in the Hamptons. The thought of being on camera felt intimidating–after all, she had never imagined herself as a television personality. Cooking had always been something she loved, but sharing it with millions of viewers in such a public way seemed daunting.

Ina hesitated for some time, unsure if she could handle the demands of television. It wasn't just a fear of being on camera–she also worried that taking on this new challenge might disrupt the personal balance she cherished. However, those closest to her, especially Jeffrey, encouraged her to take the leap. They believed that her warmth, authenticity, and relaxed approach to cooking would resonate with viewers just as they had with readers of her cookbooks. Their confidence helped Ina begin to see the opportunity not as a disruption but as an exciting new chapter.

When Ina finally agreed to give television a try, she made one thing clear: she needed creative control to ensure the show stayed true to her style. She wanted to maintain the same simplicity and authenticity that had made her cookbooks so successful. With her input, the production team agreed to film the show in her own kitchen, allowing Ina to feel comfortable and natural in front of the camera. This setting not only reflected her personality but also set the tone for *Barefoot Contessa*.

In 2002, *Barefoot Contessa* premiered, introducing Ina to an entirely new audience. From the very first episode, it was clear that Ina had made the right choice. Her easygoing manner and straightforward approach to cooking captivated viewers, making them feel like they were cooking alongside a friend. What had initially been a reluctant leap turned into a joyful, fulfilling experience, marking the beginning of Ina's rise as one of the most beloved figures in food television. The decision to say yes to the Food Network offer wasn't just a career move–it was the first step toward building a lasting legacy, one that would inspire millions of home cooks around the world.

Behind the Scenes: Building the World of *Barefoot Contessa*

Creating a successful television show required more than just great recipes–it was about crafting an experience that felt personal, inviting, and authentic. Ina Garten understood this from the start and worked closely with her production team to ensure that *Barefoot Contessa* reflected her unique style. One of her key decisions was to film the show in her real kitchen, a choice that instantly set the tone for the series. By welcoming viewers into her home, Ina made them feel like they were part of her world. This setting reinforced the authenticity that had become a hallmark of her brand, blurring the lines between everyday cooking and a lifestyle worth aspiring to.

Every episode of *Barefoot Contessa* was thoughtfully crafted to showcase not only Ina's recipes but also her philosophy on food and entertaining. The episodes followed a loose narrative structure, often revolving around themes like dinner parties, weekend brunches, or cozy meals for two. Each storyline allowed Ina to share both her cooking techniques and her personal tips for hosting and enjoying food with loved ones. Whether she was teaching viewers how to create a perfect roast chicken or offering advice on setting an elegant table, Ina made it clear that good food was about more than just ingredients–it was about creating joyful moments.

Ina's on-screen presence also contributed to the show's success. While it took time for her to feel comfortable in front of the camera, she quickly discovered that being herself was the key to connecting with her audience. Rather than adopting a polished TV persona, she embraced her natural warmth and easygoing demeanor. This authenticity made viewers feel like they were cooking alongside a friend rather than following a strict cooking lesson. Ina's ability to maintain this relaxed atmosphere, even with a production crew in the background, was a testament to her collaborative spirit. She worked closely with her team to ensure that every episode ran smoothly, creating a positive working environment that fostered creativity and consistency.

The structure of the show also reflected Ina's preference for simplicity. She avoided overly scripted scenes and allowed the episodes to flow naturally, mirroring the way she approached cooking at home. This flexibility gave the show a casual charm that resonated with viewers. Moments with Jeffrey, whether she was preparing a surprise dinner for him or sharing a laugh over a simple meal, became fan favorites, adding a personal touch to each episode.

Through thoughtful production choices, collaborative teamwork, and Ina's natural warmth, *Barefoot Contessa* became more than just a cooking show–it became a reflection of Ina's philosophy on food and life. Each episode invited viewers not only to try new recipes but also to embrace the joy of cooking and entertaining in a way that felt achievable and fun. Behind the scenes, the success of the show lay in the seamless integration of Ina's personality, culinary expertise, and collaborative spirit, creating a world that millions of viewers loved and returned to season after season.

The Appeal of Simplicity: Connecting with Audiences Worldwide

Ina Garten's approach to food, with its emphasis on simplicity and elegance, quickly set *Barefoot Contessa* apart from other cooking shows. From the outset, her focus was on making cooking accessible and enjoyable, offering recipes that anyone could recreate at home. Rather than featuring elaborate, restaurant-style meals, Ina's recipes highlighted everyday ingredients and uncomplicated techniques. This straightforward approach made viewers feel empowered to try new dishes, even if they weren't experienced in the kitchen. Ina's reassuring tone and clear instructions broke down any sense of intimidation, allowing her audience to connect with her and feel confident in their cooking abilities.

At the heart of Ina's success was her ability to make viewers feel like part of her world. She cultivated a sense of friendship with her audience, and many fans described the experience of watching *Barefoot Contessa* as akin to visiting a friend's kitchen. Her warm, relaxed demeanor—combined with her use of practical tips and personal anecdotes—added an intimacy that resonated deeply. Whether sharing shortcuts for entertaining or teaching a foolproof way to make roast chicken, Ina framed cooking as something joyful, rather than a chore to be dreaded.

A significant part of the show's charm came from the glimpses Ina shared of her personal life. The inclusion of Jeffrey, her husband, gave viewers insight into their loving relationship and brought humor and warmth to many episodes. Fans enjoyed moments when Ina would prepare meals for Jeffrey or surprise him with a special treat, adding a personal touch to the recipes. These moments, both tender and playful, endeared the couple to viewers, further deepening their connection with the show.

Ina's ability to inspire lifestyle aspirations without alienating her audience was another key to her success. Her elegant Hamptons home, beautifully set tables, and carefully curated menus offered viewers a glimpse of a life filled with beauty and hospitality. Yet Ina's charm lay in making this lifestyle feel achievable. She invited viewers to embrace the pleasure of simple things—whether hosting friends for lunch, baking cookies, or setting a welcoming table for dinner. Her philosophy was rooted in the idea that good food and good company were what mattered most, and her audience responded to that message.

Over the years, this connection with viewers only grew stronger. Ina's consistency in tone, quality, and authenticity kept her audience engaged, and the show became a beloved staple for home cooks. Fans felt that Ina's warmth and encouragement extended beyond the screen, giving them the confidence to try new things and enjoy cooking as a creative and meaningful experience. Through *Barefoot Contessa*, Ina built not just a following, but a community of viewers who saw her not just as a television host, but as a friend and mentor in the kitchen.

Balancing Fame and Privacy: Staying Grounded Amid Success

As *Barefoot Contessa* gained popularity and Ina Garten's public profile expanded, maintaining a balance between fame and privacy became increasingly important. While Ina appreciated the opportunity to connect with her audience and share her passion for cooking, she was intentional about protecting her personal life. Unlike many public figures who embrace the media spotlight fully, Ina made a conscious decision to keep significant aspects of her world off-camera. This careful boundary-setting allowed her to preserve the grounded, private lifestyle she cherished and ensured that fame did not disrupt her well-being.

One of the ways Ina managed this balance was by being selective about media engagements. Rather than chasing constant publicity, she limited interviews, endorsements, and public appearances, focusing only on projects that aligned with her values. For Ina, quality always mattered more than quantity. Each partnership, event, or project was carefully chosen to reflect the authenticity at the heart of her brand. This intentional approach kept her from becoming overexposed and ensured that her presence in the public sphere remained meaningful.

Staying true to herself amid the pressures of fame was another key aspect of Ina's success. She resisted the temptation to conform to industry trends or adopt a glamorous persona. Instead, she remained the same warm, approachable figure that viewers had come to love–focused on simple meals, personal connections, and joyful living. Her authenticity became a cornerstone of her brand, setting her apart from others in the culinary world. Fans appreciated that Ina stayed grounded, and this consistency only strengthened their trust in her over time.

Ina's focus on balance extended to her personal well-being and relationships. Throughout her career, she prioritized her marriage with Jeffrey, ensuring that their time together remained sacred. She also made sure to carve out moments for herself, taking time to recharge away from the demands of television and public life. These deliberate choices allowed her to manage the challenges of fame while continuing to produce high-quality work that reflected her passion for food and hospitality.

Ultimately, Ina's ability to balance fame with privacy contributed to her longevity in the culinary world. By staying selective and true to her values, she avoided burnout and maintained the joyful spirit that had defined her career from the beginning. This balance ensured that her work–whether in cookbooks, television, or public appearances–remained fresh, genuine, and inspiring. Fans felt connected not only to her recipes but also to the way she lived her life, which embodied the idea that success is not just about achievement but also about maintaining what truly matters.

The Evolution of *Barefoot Contessa*: Staying True While Adapting to Change

As *Barefoot Contessa* gained momentum, Ina Garten faced the challenge of maintaining the heart and soul of the show while also adapting to new trends and audience preferences. From its very first episode, the show was built on simplicity, elegance, and authenticity. Ina's ability to connect with viewers through her warm, approachable style set her apart from many other food television personalities. However, with the culinary landscape constantly evolving, *Barefoot Contessa* had to grow alongside it without losing the essence that made it special.

One of the key factors in the show's long-lasting success was its consistency in tone and quality. Even as new episodes and seasons were produced, the structure and atmosphere remained familiar. Filming continued in Ina's home kitchen, reinforcing the idea that the show was not just about food–it was about her lifestyle and the joy of cooking at home. Fans found comfort in the familiarity of each episode, with Ina preparing meals for friends or crafting something special for Jeffrey. This continuity created a sense of reliability that viewers loved, making the show feel like a visit with an old friend.

While the foundation of *Barefoot Contessa* stayed the same, the show evolved to reflect shifting culinary trends and changing viewer needs.

Ina expanded her repertoire to include more accessible weeknight meals, gluten-free options, and seasonal favorites, ensuring that her content remained relevant. She also adapted to the rise of social media, sharing tips and behind-the-scenes glimpses to connect with a broader audience. Special holiday-themed episodes and entertaining-focused content added variety, while still aligning with her philosophy of keeping things simple and joyful.

Ina's willingness to embrace small changes while staying true to her brand allowed her to remain fresh and inspiring. Fans appreciated that the show never lost its charm, even as the food world around it became more fast-paced and trend-driven. Rather than chasing fads, Ina leaned into timeless ideas–quality ingredients, easy-to-follow recipes, and the pleasure of cooking for loved ones. This consistency made her show a staple on the Food Network for over two decades, with new generations of viewers discovering the magic of *Barefoot Contessa.*

Throughout the evolution of the show, Ina also remained committed to sharing personal moments, which further deepened her connection with her audience. Her playful interactions with Jeffrey, leisurely walks through her garden, or glimpses of her entertaining friends made viewers feel like they were part of her life. These personal touches added warmth to the show and reinforced its authenticity, keeping viewers engaged and emotionally connected.

By maintaining the core values that defined *Barefoot Contessa* from the beginning–simplicity, elegance, and authenticity–Ina created a show that endured through changing times. The evolution of the series reflected her ability to adapt while staying true to herself, ensuring that both the show and her brand remained beloved across generations. In every episode, Ina continued to show that cooking doesn't have to be complicated to be meaningful, proving that sometimes the simplest things are the most satisfying.

CHAPTER 6

LOVE AND PARTNERSHIP: LIFE WITH JEFFREY

At the heart of Ina Garten's success story is her enduring relationship with Jeffrey Garten, her husband, best friend, and biggest supporter. Their love story, spanning more than five decades, has been a constant source of joy and stability in Ina's life. While Ina's talents as a chef, author, and television personality have undoubtedly shaped her career, Jeffrey's unwavering support has been equally crucial to her journey. Together, they have built a life rooted in love, respect, and partnership, balancing the demands of their individual careers while nurturing a deep personal connection.

Their love story began in the 1960s when Jeffrey first saw a photograph of Ina and knew he had to meet her. What followed was a courtship filled with letters, phone calls, and weekends spent together as they navigated young adulthood and the challenges of a long-distance relationship. From the start, Jeffrey believed in Ina's abilities, encouraging her to pursue her passions and take bold risks. His support was instrumental when Ina left her government job to open the Barefoot Contessa store, a decision that set the stage for her later success as a cookbook author and TV personality.

Throughout their marriage, they have managed to stay deeply connected, even during busy periods when Jeffrey's work as an academic and international finance expert took him far from home. They've maintained their bond through rituals like daily phone calls, shared meals, and quality time at their East Hampton home–a sanctuary that has become an integral part of Ina's public brand.

Ina and Jeffrey's relationship is more than just a marriage–it is a partnership built on mutual admiration, humor, and shared experiences. Their story serves as an inspiring example of how love and support can empower personal growth and professional success, creating a life that is as meaningful as it is joyful.

A Love Story for the Ages: The Beginnings of Ina and Jeffrey's Relationship

Ina and Jeffrey Garten's love story is one for the ages, built on a foundation of mutual admiration and deep affection. Their story began in the 1960s when Jeffrey first saw a photograph of Ina. At the time, Jeffrey was attending Dartmouth College, and the moment he saw her picture–shown to him by a friend–he was captivated. He knew immediately that he wanted to meet her. Jeffrey's determination would mark the beginning of a romance that would last a lifetime.

Their early courtship was filled with letters, phone calls, and weekends spent together whenever they could. Ina was still a student at Syracuse University, so much of their relationship had to be conducted over long distances. But Jeffrey was persistent. His charm, intelligence, and warmth drew Ina in, and their connection deepened with every interaction. Despite the challenges of being apart, the two remained committed to each other, laying the foundation for a lifelong bond.

In 1968, shortly after Ina graduated, the couple married and began adjusting to life as newlyweds. Like many young couples, they faced the joys and uncertainties of starting a new life together. Money was tight in the beginning, but they built a happy life through shared meals, laughter, and the excitement of being partners. Their ability to navigate these early years with grace set the tone for the rest of their marriage.

However, life wasn't always easy. Jeffrey's military service, which included a posting in Thailand, meant that the couple had to spend long periods apart. Later, Jeffrey's demanding career in government, finance, and academia often required him to travel extensively. But distance never weakened their bond. Through letters, phone calls, and occasional visits, they found ways to stay connected, always prioritizing their relationship despite the challenges. Ina supported Jeffrey's ambitions while he, in turn, encouraged her to pursue her own dreams, including her shift from government work to the food world.

The key to their enduring relationship lies in the qualities that have defined it from the beginning: open communication, humor, and unwavering admiration for each other. Even in the most demanding times, they made a point of talking daily, sharing their thoughts and lives with one another. Humor has been another essential ingredient in their marriage. They never took themselves too seriously, and their ability to laugh together—whether over a simple meal or during life's stressful moments—helped them maintain perspective.

Above all, their relationship has always been marked by respect and encouragement. From their early days as newlyweds to the later years as established professionals, they have supported one another's ambitions while cherishing their time together. This mutual admiration, combined with a deep friendship, has allowed Ina and Jeffrey to build a life that is as meaningful as it is joyful. Their love story is not just about romance—it's about partnership, trust, and the shared belief that life is best when enjoyed together.

Jeffrey's Influence on Ina's Career: Encouraging Her to Dream Big

Jeffrey Garten has been a constant source of support and encouragement throughout Ina's career, playing a crucial role in helping her pursue her passion for food. In the 1970s, Ina was working in a government job at the Office of Management and Budget, focusing on energy policy. While the work was secure and respectable, Ina began to feel unfulfilled. She loved cooking for friends on weekends, hosting dinner parties, and experimenting with new recipes, but making food her career felt like a distant dream. Jeffrey, however, saw her potential from the beginning. He encouraged Ina to leave behind the safety of her government career and take a bold leap toward what she truly loved. His belief in her talent was unwavering and gave her the confidence to take the first step.

It was Jeffrey's encouragement that ultimately led Ina to buy the Barefoot Contessa specialty food store in East Hampton. Although the decision came with significant risks—leaving behind a stable job and entering an industry where she had no formal experience—Jeffrey assured her that it was worth pursuing. He believed in Ina's natural gift for cooking and hospitality, and he trusted that her passion would guide her. His emotional support during those early days of uncertainty gave Ina the courage to navigate the steep learning curve of running a business.

Even as Ina's career evolved beyond the Barefoot Contessa store, Jeffrey remained her biggest supporter. When Ina transitioned to writing cookbooks and hosting her television show, Jeffrey was always there, cheering her on from the sidelines. Whether it was helping her celebrate a successful book launch or offering words of encouragement when things felt overwhelming, Jeffrey provided the steady support that Ina needed. During filming for *Barefoot Contessa*, Jeffrey's playful appearances on the show became a fan-favorite feature, showcasing the deep bond they shared.

Jeffrey's own career in international finance and academia also shaped their life together. His roles–first in the U.S. government and later as the dean of Yale's School of Management–often required extensive travel, but rather than causing strain, these experiences enriched their relationship. The couple embraced a lifestyle that balanced Jeffrey's professional demands with their shared love of food, travel, and time together at their East Hampton home. Ina's ability to build her career was, in part, made possible by Jeffrey's trust and the freedom they gave each other to pursue their individual ambitions.

At the core of their relationship is a deep sense of equality and respect. Jeffrey never sought to overshadow Ina's achievements but instead celebrated them wholeheartedly. Their marriage has always been a partnership in the truest sense–one where both partners support and uplift each other's goals. Jeffrey's belief in Ina's potential has allowed her to take risks and build a career that brings her joy, while his steady presence has ensured that she never feels alone on her journey. Their story is not just one of personal love but also a testament to the power of mutual support in building a fulfilling and successful life.

Balancing Marriage and Career: Building an Empire While Maintaining a Strong Partnership

Ina Garten's career flourished over the decades, evolving from a small specialty food store owner to a bestselling cookbook author and beloved television personality. While building her culinary empire required dedication and long hours, Ina never lost sight of what mattered most–her marriage with Jeffrey. Balancing an ambitious career with a strong, loving partnership took intention and effort, especially as both Ina and Jeffrey juggled demanding professional lives. Through it all, they found ways to stay connected, maintain their bond, and ensure that their relationship remained a priority.

One of the biggest challenges the couple faced was time spent apart. Jeffrey's career as an academic and international finance expert often required extensive travel, especially during his years teaching at Yale and working overseas. There were periods when Jeffrey spent days or even weeks away from home. Instead of letting the distance strain their relationship, Ina and Jeffrey made conscious efforts to stay connected. They spoke on the phone every day, no matter where Jeffrey was, sharing details about their lives and offering each other encouragement. These daily conversations became a cherished ritual, reinforcing their emotional connection and sense of partnership.

Ina and Jeffrey also prioritized quality time together whenever possible, creating traditions that strengthened their relationship. Weekend dinners became a sacred time for them to reconnect, with Ina often cooking Jeffrey's favorite meals. Whether they were hosting friends or enjoying a quiet night at home, their shared love of food and entertaining provided a foundation for their time together. Ina's habit of surprising Jeffrey with special meals on the show–like a romantic dinner or a picnic–wasn't just for television; it reflected the thoughtful gestures that have always been a part of their relationship.

Jeffrey's role in Ina's public life added another layer to the balance between marriage and career. His playful appearances on *Barefoot Contessa* became a fan-favorite element of the show, offering viewers a glimpse into their loving relationship. These moments weren't scripted–they were genuine reflections of their dynamic, filled with humor, affection, and mutual respect. The way Jeffrey admired Ina on-screen was the same way he supported her behind the scenes, celebrating her achievements without ever seeking to overshadow her. Their relationship became an essential part of Ina's brand, symbolizing the joy of shared experiences, whether cooking a meal or spending time together.

Despite their public success, Ina and Jeffrey have always maintained a sense of privacy and balance. While Ina's career demanded a great deal of her time, she made a conscious effort to protect her personal life, setting boundaries that allowed her to nurture her relationship with Jeffrey. Similarly, Jeffrey's support made it possible for Ina to pursue her passion without guilt or resentment. Their ability to respect each other's ambitions while staying emotionally connected has been key to maintaining both a thriving career and a fulfilling marriage.

Ina and Jeffrey's story illustrates the power of partnership in both personal and professional life. They have shown that love and ambition don't have to be at odds–in fact, with the right balance, they can complement each other. Their marriage, built on communication, humor, and mutual respect, is not just a backdrop to Ina's career–it has been a driving force behind her success, allowing her to build an empire while keeping the joy of partnership at the center of it all.

Life in East Hampton: A Home That Reflects Their Love and Partnership

For Ina and Jeffrey Garten, East Hampton is more than just a picturesque getaway–it is the heart of their shared life and a sanctuary where their relationship flourishes. When they first purchased their Hamptons home in the 1970s, they intended it to be a peaceful retreat from the hectic pace of life in New York City. Over the years, it has evolved into much more: a place where Ina found inspiration for her culinary career, where Jeffrey found respite from his academic and professional work, and where they nurtured their bond through simple pleasures like cooking, entertaining, and enjoying time together.

Their home in East Hampton is a reflection of their partnership, blending Ina's love for food and entertaining with Jeffrey's appreciation for comfort and tranquility. They both worked together to create a space that felt welcoming and serene–a place that aligned with their shared values of simplicity and joy. From the sprawling garden where Ina harvests fresh herbs and vegetables for her recipes to the cozy dining table where they enjoy their meals, every corner of their home tells the story of their life together.

A typical day in their East Hampton life involves quiet routines that have become treasured rituals. Ina loves to prepare meals for Jeffrey, often testing new recipes or perfecting old favorites in her kitchen. Jeffrey, for his part, delights in her cooking, always greeting her creations with genuine enthusiasm–a dynamic that has become a beloved part of Ina's brand. Their weekends often involve long walks along the beach, gardening, or sharing coffee on the patio, relishing the simple joys that come with being together. These seemingly ordinary moments have helped them stay connected and grounded, despite their busy professional lives.

The life they have built in East Hampton has become an integral part of Ina's public image, inspiring many of the recipes, stories, and themes that appear in her cookbooks and television shows. Fans of *Barefoot Contessa* often get glimpses of the couple's life there, with episodes filmed in Ina's home kitchen and garden. These elements offer a sense of authenticity that resonates deeply with viewers, who see Ina and Jeffrey's relationship as a model of enduring love and partnership. The ease and joy with which they live their lives in the Hamptons embody the core of Ina's brand: the idea that good food, shared experiences, and a comfortable home are the foundations of a happy life.

Despite their public presence, Ina and Jeffrey have remained grounded in the simplicity of their East Hampton lifestyle. Their ability to maintain a private, meaningful life together while pursuing ambitious careers is a testament to the strength of their partnership. East Hampton offers them a place to disconnect from the demands of the outside world and focus on what matters most: their relationship. Whether cooking a meal together, enjoying a quiet evening, or welcoming friends into their home, Ina and Jeffrey have found a way to turn their shared life in East Hampton into a reflection of everything they value–love, joy, and the pleasure of being together.

The Secret to Lasting Love: Reflections on Their Relationship After Decades Together

Ina and Jeffrey Garten's relationship has spanned over five decades, a testament to their deep love, mutual respect, and commitment to one another. Their marriage has not only stood the test of time but has thrived, serving as an inspiration to many fans and followers. While no relationship is without its challenges, Ina and Jeffrey have navigated the highs and lows of life together with humor, trust, and a shared appreciation for each other's individuality. Their love story demonstrates that lasting relationships are built on friendship, communication, and intentional effort.

One of the secrets to their enduring marriage is their ability to support and celebrate each other's successes. Throughout their marriage, Jeffrey has been Ina's biggest cheerleader, offering unwavering support as she transitioned from government work to running a food store, then to writing cookbooks and becoming a television personality. Similarly, Ina has supported Jeffrey's demanding career in academia and international finance, giving him the freedom to travel and pursue his passions. Their mutual encouragement has allowed them both to grow as individuals while remaining deeply connected as partners.

Humor has also been a cornerstone of their relationship. Ina and Jeffrey both emphasize the importance of not taking life–or each other–too seriously. Their playful dynamic, often captured on *Barefoot Contessa*, offers viewers a glimpse into their shared sense of humor, which has kept their relationship light and joyful even during stressful times. This ability to laugh together has been a key ingredient in sustaining their bond over the years.

Another essential element of their marriage is communication. Whether through phone calls during Jeffrey's travels or conversations over meals, they have always made time to connect, sharing the small and big moments of their lives. They have developed a habit of expressing gratitude for one another, never taking their relationship for granted. These intentional acts of communication have kept their connection strong, even when life's demands pulled them in different directions.

Their relationship is also marked by a deep respect for each other's independence. Rather than seeing time apart as a threat to their marriage, they embraced it as an opportunity to pursue their individual passions. This balance of togetherness and independence has allowed them to maintain a healthy relationship without sacrificing their personal growth. They understand that a strong partnership is not about being inseparable but about supporting each other's dreams while cherishing the time they spend together.

As they reflect on their life together, Ina and Jeffrey focus on gratitude and the joy of shared experiences. They celebrate each other's successes, laugh at life's small quirks, and cherish the everyday moments that make their relationship meaningful. For them, the key to a happy marriage lies in the little things—like enjoying a meal together, walking along the beach, or sitting quietly with a cup of coffee. Their story is a reminder that true love is not about grand gestures but about consistently showing up for one another, day after day, year after year.

Ina and Jeffrey's marriage is more than just a love story—it's a partnership built on trust, laughter, and mutual respect. Their ability to balance career, love, and personal growth serves as an example that lasting relationships are not about perfection but about choosing each other every day. As they continue to share their journey with the world, Ina and Jeffrey show that love, when nurtured with care and intention, only grows stronger with time.

CHAPTER 7

COOKBOOKS AND CULINARY LEGACY

Ina Garten's cookbooks are more than collections of recipes–they are windows into her philosophy of food, hospitality, and joyful living. Over the course of her career, Ina has written numerous bestselling cookbooks, each one building on the principles that made her debut so successful: simplicity, elegance, and reliability. These books, filled with accessible yet delicious recipes, have cemented her reputation as one of the most beloved culinary figures of our time. With a writing style that feels both personal and practical, Ina has made home cooking approachable for countless readers around the world.

The success of her first cookbook, *The Barefoot Contessa Cookbook*, laid the foundation for her career as a culinary icon. What started as a way to share the most popular dishes from her East Hampton store with a wider audience quickly became a bestseller. The book's friendly tone, clear instructions, and foolproof recipes resonated with home cooks, proving that great meals didn't have to be complicated. It set the tone for the books that followed, establishing a blueprint for how Ina would blend personal stories, practical cooking advice, and entertaining tips into her writing.

Ina's approach to writing cookbooks is rooted in her belief that food should be joyful, not intimidating. Whether teaching readers how to roast the perfect chicken or offering advice on stress-free entertaining, Ina writes with warmth and simplicity, as if she's guiding a friend through the kitchen. Each recipe undergoes meticulous testing to ensure it will work perfectly every time, reinforcing the trust that readers place in her.

Beyond the pages of her cookbooks, Ina has left an indelible mark on the way people cook and entertain. Her emphasis on quality ingredients, straightforward techniques, and relaxed gatherings has reshaped modern home cooking. Ina's culinary legacy extends beyond her recipes–she has influenced the way people think about food, host guests, and enjoy the everyday pleasures of life.

The Success of the First Cookbook: Setting the Foundation for a Culinary Icon

When Ina Garten decided to write *The Barefoot Contessa Cookbook*, it marked the beginning of an unexpected yet transformative journey. After selling her specialty food store in East Hampton, Ina found herself searching for a new direction. The store had been a place where she could express her love for cooking and entertaining, and she didn't want to leave that world behind entirely. Writing a cookbook offered a way to capture the essence of the Barefoot Contessa store and share it with a broader audience. At first, Ina was unsure if she could translate her passion for food into a book, but with Jeffrey's encouragement, she embraced the opportunity. Her goal was simple: to create a collection of recipes that reflected the approachable, delicious food her customers had loved for years.

Crafting the introduction to her debut cookbook was just as important to Ina as the recipes themselves. She wanted the book to feel personal, as though readers were sitting with her at the kitchen table, chatting about food and life. Ina used personal anecdotes and stories to connect with readers from the outset, sharing memories of her time running the Barefoot Contessa store and offering insights into her philosophy on food. Her warm, friendly tone made the book feel inviting, encouraging even the most hesitant home cooks to give her recipes a try.

The response to *The Barefoot Contessa Cookbook* was immediate and overwhelming. Published in 1999, the book became an instant bestseller, earning critical acclaim for its clarity, simplicity, and charm. Ina's recipes were praised for being foolproof–approachable enough for beginners yet satisfying enough for experienced cooks. At a time when many cookbooks were either overly complex or hyper-specialized, Ina's straightforward approach stood out. She emphasized fresh, high-quality ingredients, simple techniques, and the joy of cooking for others, which resonated deeply with readers. Home cooks appreciated that her recipes worked exactly as promised, building trust and loyalty from the start.

The success of her first cookbook not only solidified Ina's reputation as a culinary authority but also set the tone for her future work. The positive reception gave her the confidence to pursue additional projects, leading to the creation of more bestselling cookbooks. Each subsequent book followed a similar formula–delicious, uncomplicated food paired with Ina's friendly voice and practical tips for entertaining–allowing her to build a brand rooted in authenticity and accessibility.

More than two decades later, *The Barefoot Contessa Cookbook* remains a beloved classic. It not only captured the spirit of Ina's food store but also introduced readers to her unique approach to cooking and entertaining. The book's success laid the foundation for a career that would span cookbooks, television, and more, turning Ina Garten into one of the most trusted and admired figures in the culinary world.

Writing from the Heart: Crafting Cookbooks that Resonate

Ina Garten's cookbooks stand out not only for their delicious recipes but for the heart and thoughtfulness she puts into every page. From the beginning, Ina's approach to writing cookbooks has been rooted in her desire to make cooking accessible, joyful, and satisfying. For her, food isn't just about sustenance–it's about creating experiences and connecting with others. This philosophy has guided every book she's written, ensuring her work resonates with readers at a personal level.

Ina's culinary philosophy is built on simplicity and reliability. She believes that great food doesn't need to be complicated and that every home cook should feel empowered in the kitchen. This approach is evident in all her books, where she focuses on foolproof recipes using a handful of quality ingredients. Whether it's a roast chicken, a creamy pasta dish, or a classic dessert, Ina's recipes are designed to be approachable and achievable for cooks at any skill level. She avoids overly technical techniques, emphasizing instead that good cooking is about confidence and care.

A key element of Ina's writing is her ability to blend sophistication with ease. Her recipes feel special, whether they're for a casual brunch or an elegant dinner party. She encourages readers to embrace simplicity without sacrificing flavor, demonstrating that a thoughtfully prepared meal can still feel luxurious. This balance between elegance and practicality makes her books unique—offering both everyday staples and impressive dishes for entertaining.

Ina's cookbooks are also filled with personal stories and entertaining tips, giving readers a glimpse into her life. She often shares memories from her East Hampton home, anecdotes about her relationship with Jeffrey, and advice for hosting stress-free gatherings. These elements make her books feel more like conversations with a friend than instruction manuals. Readers are not only learning how to cook but also gaining insight into Ina's life and her love for creating meaningful moments through food.

One of the most remarkable aspects of Ina's cookbooks is how they prioritize enjoyment over perfection. She believes that cooking should be fun, not intimidating. Throughout her books, she reassures readers that it's okay to make mistakes and encourages them to relax and enjoy the process. This message of ease and comfort is woven into every recipe, helping home cooks feel confident even when trying something new.

Ultimately, Ina's ability to write from the heart is what makes her books so beloved. Her warmth, sincerity, and practical advice resonate with readers, turning her cookbooks into trusted companions in kitchens around the world. Each book reflects her philosophy that food is about more than just recipes—it's about bringing joy to everyday life, sharing meals with loved ones, and celebrating the simple pleasures of cooking at home.

The Art of Recipe Testing: Ensuring Every Dish is Foolproof

One of the reasons Ina Garten's cookbooks are so beloved is her meticulous dedication to recipe testing. For Ina, a recipe isn't just a list of ingredients and instructions—it's a promise to her readers that if they follow her guidance, the dish will turn out perfectly every time.

This commitment to reliability has become a hallmark of her work, building a deep sense of trust with her audience. Ina's fans know that if a recipe appears in one of her books, it has been rigorously tested and refined to be foolproof.

Ina's approach to recipe testing is rooted in precision and thoroughness. She begins with an idea, often inspired by her travels, favorite ingredients, or meals she has prepared at home. From there, she develops the first version of the recipe, paying close attention to measurements, cooking times, and techniques. Each ingredient is carefully considered to ensure the dish is both flavorful and easy to prepare. Ina's goal is not just to create delicious food, but to make sure the recipe is achievable for home cooks of all skill levels.

Once a draft recipe is complete, the real work begins. Ina tests each dish multiple times in her home kitchen, adjusting ingredients, cooking temperatures, or methods as needed. If a step feels too complicated, she finds a way to simplify it without compromising the quality of the dish. Throughout this process, she focuses on consistency–if a recipe works perfectly one time but not the next, she continues to tweak it until the results are reliable every time. This rigorous testing process ensures that anyone, whether a novice or an experienced cook, can successfully replicate her recipes.

Ina's testing process is not a solitary endeavor. She often works closely with a small team of trusted assistants who help her test recipes. Each dish is prepared multiple times, sometimes by different people, to ensure that the instructions are clear and the results consistent. This collaborative approach ensures that her recipes are foolproof across a variety of kitchens and cooks. If any part of the recipe feels confusing or doesn't yield perfect results, it goes back to the drawing board.

Ina also places a strong emphasis on feedback. She listens carefully to the input of her testers and adjusts her recipes accordingly. Whether it's refining a sauce, altering a cooking time, or suggesting substitutions, every detail matters. This attention to feedback ensures that her recipes are as practical as they are delicious.

Through her dedication to rigorous testing, Ina has built a reputation for reliability that sets her cookbooks apart. Readers know they can count on her recipes to work exactly as written, and this trust has become one of the cornerstones of her culinary legacy. For Ina, recipe testing is not just about getting it right–it's about ensuring that every home cook feels confident and successful in the kitchen.

Building a Collection: Highlights from Her Most Popular Cookbooks

Over the years, Ina Garten has created a rich collection of cookbooks that reflect her culinary philosophy and lifestyle. Each book offers a unique blend of accessible recipes, personal stories, and practical entertaining tips. Whether teaching readers how to make weeknight dinners, holiday feasts, or simple yet elegant desserts, Ina's cookbooks consistently reflect the same warmth and reliability that have defined her career. Through these books, Ina has built a legacy that inspires generations of home cooks.

Her first cookbook, *The Barefoot Contessa Cookbook* (1999), was a resounding success and laid the foundation for her future projects. It captured the spirit of the East Hampton food store she once owned, featuring crowd-pleasing recipes like roast chicken and lemon pound cake. Its focus on simplicity and high-quality ingredients resonated with readers, establishing a blueprint for Ina's future books. This debut proved that Ina's friendly, conversational style and foolproof recipes would set her apart in the crowded culinary world.

Ina followed her first success with *Barefoot Contessa Parties!* in 2001, which emphasized her love for entertaining. This book provided readers with stress-free strategies for hosting events, with menus designed for a variety of gatherings. Ina's emphasis on enjoying the moment and not getting bogged down by perfection became a signature theme. Recipes like Parmesan crisps and make-ahead appetizers reflected her practical approach to hosting, and her tips on creating a welcoming atmosphere further cemented her reputation as an expert on elegant entertaining.

With *Barefoot Contessa at Home* (2006), Ina invited readers deeper into her personal life, offering recipes inspired by her Hamptons lifestyle. This book became one of her most beloved, focusing on the joy of everyday meals shared with family and friends. Recipes like her famous tomato and goat cheese tarts and Jeffrey's favorite roast chicken became fan favorites. The book highlighted Ina's belief that home cooking should be about creating joyful, meaningful moments rather than striving for culinary perfection.

Ina continued to evolve with *Make It Ahead* (2014), which provided busy readers with practical ways to prepare meals in advance. This book reflected Ina's understanding of modern cooking needs, showing how preparation can make entertaining stress-free. Recipes like slow-cooked beef brisket and overnight French toast demonstrated her ability to balance flavor and convenience. The book's success illustrated Ina's ability to adapt while maintaining her signature warmth and elegance.

Her more recent release, *Modern Comfort Food* (2020), was particularly timely, offering comforting recipes during a period when many people sought solace in cooking at home. Dishes like baked rigatoni with lamb ragù and cheddar and chutney grilled cheese reflected her knack for blending nostalgia with modern flavors. This cookbook, like all her others, reaffirmed Ina's ability to make cooking feel approachable, joyful, and fulfilling.

Across her entire collection, Ina's books consistently reflect the themes that have defined her career: quality ingredients, straightforward techniques, and a focus on enjoying food with loved ones. Whether offering recipes for elegant dinner parties or cozy family meals, Ina's cookbooks make readers feel capable, confident, and welcome in the kitchen. Her personal stories, thoughtful tips, and reliable instructions continue to inspire home cooks, ensuring that her influence will endure for generations.

Culinary Legacy: Shaping the Way People Cook and Entertain

Ina Garten's impact on the culinary world goes far beyond her recipes and television presence–she has transformed the way people think about cooking and entertaining. With her approachable philosophy,

Ina has made home cooking feel achievable, joyful, and meaningful. Her influence has reshaped modern kitchens, emphasizing the importance of using quality ingredients, focusing on simplicity, and creating experiences that bring people together. Ina's legacy is not just about teaching people how to cook–it's about empowering them to embrace the pleasures of food, whether preparing a weeknight dinner or hosting a special gathering.

One of Ina's most significant contributions to home cooking is her emphasis on ease and accessibility. In a world where culinary trends can often feel intimidating, Ina has consistently encouraged people to relax and enjoy the process. She has redefined what it means to entertain at home, emphasizing that it doesn't require elaborate meals or formalities. Instead, Ina promotes gatherings that are casual and fun, where the host can enjoy the company of guests without being stuck in the kitchen. Her philosophy has resonated with countless people, inspiring them to cook not for perfection, but for the pleasure of bringing loved ones together.

Ina has also helped home cooks embrace the value of high-quality ingredients. Long before "farm-to-table" became a popular buzzword, Ina was advocating for simple meals made with fresh, seasonal produce. Her recipes demonstrate how just a few good ingredients–like ripe tomatoes, fragrant herbs, or a fresh loaf of bread–can come together to create something extraordinary. This approach has inspired a generation of home cooks to move away from overly complicated dishes and focus instead on the flavors that come from thoughtful preparation and excellent ingredients.

Beyond the kitchen, Ina has transformed the way people approach entertaining. Through her cookbooks and TV show, she has shown that hosting doesn't have to be stressful–it can be enjoyable for both the guests and the host. Her make-ahead strategies, practical tips, and easygoing attitude have changed the way people think about hospitality. Ina's message is clear: the most important part of any gathering is not the food on the table, but the connections it fosters between people.

Ina's influence extends beyond individual kitchens–she has left an indelible mark on the culinary industry as a whole. She has inspired countless chefs, food writers, and lifestyle experts with her philosophy of simplicity and joy. Her work has demonstrated that food media can be both instructional and heartwarming, creating an emotional connection with audiences. Ina's ability to remain authentic and true to her values, even as trends shift, has solidified her as a trusted voice in the food world.

As Ina's cookbooks continue to inspire new generations of home cooks, her culinary legacy will endure. Through her focus on ease, quality, and enjoyment, Ina has not only shaped the way people cook and entertain but also redefined how they experience food and hospitality. Her lasting impact is a reminder that food is about more than just recipes–it's about creating moments of connection, comfort, and joy that leave lasting memories.

Ina Garten's cookbooks have left an indelible mark on the culinary world, redefining home cooking with simplicity, warmth, and elegance. Through her approachable recipes, personal stories, and entertaining tips, Ina has built a legacy of inspiring confidence in home cooks. Her meticulous recipe testing ensures reliability, creating trust with her audience that spans generations. Beyond individual kitchens, Ina has shaped the way people cook, entertain, and find joy in food. As her books continue to inspire, Ina's philosophy of quality, ease, and connection will remain a guiding force, ensuring her culinary legacy endures for years to come.

CHAPTER 8

ENTREPRENEURIAL SPIRIT: EXPANDING THE BRAND

Ina Garten's journey from food entrepreneur to lifestyle icon is a testament to her thoughtful approach to growth. What began as a specialty food store evolved into a successful career as a cookbook author and television personality. Yet, Ina's influence extends far beyond the pages of her books and the screen—over time, she has carefully cultivated a lifestyle brand that reflects her values of simplicity, elegance, and authenticity. Through strategic partnerships and selective business ventures, Ina has expanded her reach, offering more than just recipes; she provides inspiration for the way people live, entertain, and create meaningful moments at home.

The shift from food to lifestyle came naturally for Ina, whose cookbooks and television show offered more than just cooking instructions—they showcased a way of living. Fans were drawn not only to her recipes but also to the relaxed yet refined atmosphere of her East Hampton home. This aspirational lifestyle became a core part of her brand, paving the way for expansions into home goods, kitchen tools, and other products designed to reflect her philosophy of effortless elegance.

However, Ina has been deliberate about how she grows her brand, choosing partnerships and endorsements that align with her values. From cookware collections to food products, every collaboration reflects her emphasis on quality and authenticity. This careful, thoughtful approach has allowed Ina to maintain the trust and loyalty of her audience, even as she expands into new markets.

In this chapter, we explore the evolution of Ina's brand, the collaborations and ventures that extended her influence beyond food, and how she has stayed true to her identity through it all. By focusing on meaningful growth rather than chasing trends, Ina Garten has built a business empire that continues to inspire and resonate with people around the world.

From Food to Lifestyle: Evolving into a Comprehensive Brand

Ina Garten's evolution from food-focused entrepreneur to lifestyle icon happened organically over time, as she expanded her work beyond cookbooks and television. Although her initial success came from her food store, cookbooks, and TV show, Ina's brand began to encompass more than just recipes. Her audience quickly recognized that Ina's expertise extended into other areas of life, including home décor, entertaining, and thoughtful living. What started as a focus on delicious, accessible meals grew into a larger lifestyle philosophy rooted in simplicity, elegance, and warmth.

Ina's transition from food to lifestyle emerged naturally through the content of her cookbooks and television series. Both offered more than just culinary instruction–they gave fans glimpses into her personal life in East Hampton, where she and Jeffrey created a serene, inviting home. Ina's viewers and readers became captivated not only by her cooking but also by the ambiance she cultivated–stylish but unfussy décor, a comfortable kitchen, and relaxed entertaining with friends and family. The aspirational yet attainable nature of her lifestyle resonated with fans, who admired her ability to blend elegance with ease. Over time, her brand evolved to reflect not just how to cook a great meal but also how to live well.

Ina's love for entertaining played a key role in expanding her brand beyond food. From her early days running the Barefoot Contessa store, Ina understood that food was only part of a great experience; the atmosphere, décor, and thoughtful touches also mattered. Her cookbooks and TV episodes featured entertaining tips, from setting a beautiful table to creating a relaxed mood for guests. As her influence grew, so did the demand for products that reflected her signature style. Ina's focus on simple yet elegant entertaining inspired product ideas–such as kitchenware, home goods, and entertaining essentials–that aligned with her philosophy of easy sophistication.

The core of Ina's brand reflects her personal values and aesthetic. Her love for natural beauty, simplicity, and quality runs through everything she creates, from recipes to table settings. She embraces a style that feels refined but never ostentatious—one that prioritizes comfort and joy over perfection. This personal touch has been instrumental in shaping her brand identity, making her audience feel connected to her not just as a culinary expert but as someone who embodies a lifestyle they admire.

What sets Ina apart is her ability to strike the perfect balance between aspiration and accessibility. Her fans are drawn to the elegant world she has created, but they also feel empowered to recreate it in their own lives. Ina's warmth and authenticity make her lifestyle brand feel achievable, not distant or exclusive. This blend of inspiration and practicality has allowed her to expand her reach, moving effortlessly beyond food into a broader lifestyle brand that continues to resonate with audiences worldwide.

Collaborations and Partnerships: Expanding Through Strategic Alliances

Ina Garten's brand expansion has also been fueled by strategic collaborations and partnerships that align with her core philosophy. As her audience grew, opportunities arose to create products that reflected her style and extended her influence beyond cookbooks and television. However, unlike many public figures who rush into endorsements, Ina has taken a thoughtful and selective approach to partnerships. Each collaboration has been carefully chosen to complement her brand values of simplicity, elegance, and quality.

Ina's product partnerships have focused primarily on items that support her love for cooking, entertaining, and living well. Kitchenware, cookware, and tableware collections have been natural extensions of her brand, giving her fans the tools to replicate her style in their own homes. These collaborations reflect her belief that well-designed, functional items enhance the experience of cooking and entertaining. Ina has also ventured into food products, curating high-quality ingredients such as olive oil, condiments, and pantry staples—items that align with her philosophy of using the best ingredients to create simple but delicious meals.

Selectivity has been a key factor in Ina's approach to partnerships. Rather than spreading herself thin with numerous endorsements, she has chosen collaborations that feel authentic and aligned with her values. This careful curation reinforces the trust she has built with her audience, who know that every product associated with her name meets her high standards. Ina's selectivity has also preserved the exclusivity and integrity of her brand, making her products highly desirable to consumers.

In addition to product collaborations, Ina has participated in media engagements and public appearances that enhance her brand's reach. However, she remains deliberate in her choices, avoiding overexposure while ensuring that each event aligns with her message of joyful, stress-free living. Whether promoting a new cookbook or attending a food festival, Ina's presence is always consistent with her brand's core identity.

Ina's partnerships have also opened new doors, allowing her to expand into markets beyond the kitchen. Her influence now extends to home décor, entertaining essentials, and lifestyle products that reflect the same easy elegance she embodies in her personal life. By venturing into these areas, Ina has been able to connect with audiences on a deeper level, inspiring not just how people cook but how they live.

Ultimately, Ina's collaborations and partnerships are more than business ventures—they are extensions of her brand philosophy. Every product she endorses or creates reflects her commitment to quality, simplicity, and joy. By staying selective and intentional in her partnerships, Ina has expanded her influence without compromising her authenticity, cementing her status as a trusted and beloved lifestyle icon.

Maintaining Authenticity: Staying True to the Brand While Growing

Throughout her career, Ina Garten has remained true to the core values that define her brand: simplicity, quality, and joy. As her business ventures expanded beyond cookbooks and television, she carefully ensured that each new project reflected these principles. From the food she creates to the products she endorses, Ina's work has consistently embodied a philosophy of thoughtful living. Her emphasis on authenticity and consistency has been central to building a brand that resonates deeply with her audience, allowing her to grow without compromising her identity.

Every venture Ina undertakes aligns with the core values she established from the start. Whether launching a new cookbook, developing product lines, or entering partnerships, she applies the same attention to detail and passion for quality. Her focus on simplicity is evident in everything she does–recipes feature a few well-chosen ingredients, cookware designs are functional yet elegant, and entertaining tips promote ease over extravagance. This consistency allows her audience to trust that whatever bears her name will meet the same high standards they have come to expect.

Ina has also avoided the pitfalls of overexpansion by taking a cautious approach to business growth. She prioritizes projects that align with her vision rather than chasing trends or pursuing ventures for the sake of profit. While many public figures jump at every endorsement opportunity, Ina remains selective about the products and media engagements she takes on. This measured approach preserves the exclusivity and integrity of her brand. Fans know that anything Ina endorses or creates reflects her personal values, reinforcing their loyalty and trust.

Staying connected with her audience has been essential to maintaining authenticity. Despite her growing empire, Ina cultivates personal connections with her fans through newsletters, social media, and personal anecdotes. On Instagram, she offers behind-the-scenes glimpses into her life, shares new recipes, and provides words of encouragement. Her newsletters feel like letters from a friend, offering entertaining tips and ideas for seasonal meals. This personal touch keeps her audience engaged and strengthens the sense of community around her brand.

Ina's ability to maintain authenticity while growing her brand is a testament to her commitment to thoughtful, intentional work. Every new venture is carefully considered, ensuring it aligns with her philosophy of joy, simplicity, and quality. By resisting overexpansion, focusing on meaningful projects, and nurturing personal connections with her audience, Ina has built a lasting brand that continues to inspire. In an ever-evolving marketplace, her authenticity sets her apart and ensures that her influence will endure for years to come.

Challenges and Learning Curves: Navigating Expansion and Growth

Expanding a brand beyond its original scope comes with challenges, and Ina Garten's journey was no exception. As she ventured beyond cookbooks and television, she faced new learning curves in unfamiliar markets. Navigating product partnerships, developing new business strategies, and maintaining her brand's integrity required careful thought and adjustments. However, Ina's thoughtful approach to these challenges has been central to her ability to sustain long-term success.

One of the first challenges Ina encountered was learning how to extend her brand beyond food without diluting its core identity. While her cookbooks and TV show focused on food and entertaining, her foray into home goods, cookware, and other products required a new skill set. Ina had to learn how to collaborate with designers and manufacturers to ensure the quality of the products matched her standards. She also had to figure out how to maintain the authenticity of her brand as it evolved into new categories. This transition required adjustments, but Ina's dedication to quality and simplicity helped her navigate these changes successfully.

Balancing business growth with personal life presented another challenge. As Ina's brand expanded, the demands on her time increased. With new cookbooks to write, media appearances to manage, and product partnerships to oversee, maintaining her personal life and relationship with Jeffrey became increasingly important. Ina has always emphasized the need to set boundaries, focusing only on projects that bring her joy and align with her values. Her ability to say no to opportunities that don't fit her vision has allowed her to maintain a sense of balance, ensuring that her business ventures never come at the expense of her personal well-being.

Ina's relationship with Jeffrey has been a cornerstone of her ability to manage the challenges of growth. Despite their busy schedules, the couple makes time for each other, prioritizing their relationship above all else. They maintain daily rituals, such as phone calls and shared meals, which provide stability amid the demands of business. This focus on balance has allowed Ina to pursue her ambitions without compromising her personal life.

Through trial and error, Ina has learned that sustainable growth requires thoughtful decisions and flexibility. She has adjusted her strategies over the years, ensuring that her brand stays relevant while remaining true to her identity. Rather than rushing into new ventures, Ina takes the time to assess whether each opportunity aligns with her values and long-term vision. This patient, intentional approach has allowed her to overcome the challenges of expansion while preserving the joy and authenticity that define her brand.

Ina's journey offers valuable lessons in navigating business growth. Her ability to maintain balance, embrace learning curves, and stay true to her values serves as an example of how thoughtful, deliberate choices can lead to long-lasting success.

Ina's legacy extends beyond her business ventures—it lies in the inspiration she has provided to countless individuals who admire her philosophy of effortless elegance. Home cooks have learned from her that cooking should be joyful and accessible. Aspiring entrepreneurs have looked to her as a model of how to build a brand with intention, focusing on meaningful growth rather than chasing trends. Hosts and entertainers have embraced her idea that hospitality is not about impressing guests, but about creating moments of connection. Ina's thoughtful approach has encouraged people to savor life's small pleasures, from cooking a comforting meal to setting a beautiful table.

In an increasingly fast-paced world, Ina's brand serves as a model for sustainable, authentic business growth. Her careful approach to expansion—focusing only on projects that align with her values—stands in contrast to the rapid, trend-driven growth pursued by many companies today. Ina's ability to maintain authenticity while adapting to new opportunities offers a valuable lesson: success comes from staying true to what matters most. As her influence continues to grow,

Ina Garten's brand will remain a beacon of inspiration, proving that thoughtful, meaningful work can create a lasting impact.

Ina Garten's journey from cookbook author to lifestyle icon reflects her thoughtful approach to business and personal growth. By expanding her brand into new ventures–ranging from home goods to entertaining essentials–while staying true to her values of simplicity, quality, and authenticity, Ina has built an empire that resonates with audiences worldwide. Her selective partnerships, personal connection with fans, and focus on meaningful growth have made her a model for sustainable success. As her brand continues to evolve, Ina's legacy will remain a powerful example of how thoughtful, intentional work can create lasting influence in both business and life.

CHAPTER 9

PERSONAL CHALLENGES AND TRIUMPHS

Behind Ina Garten's polished success lies a story of challenges, setbacks, and personal growth. While she has become a beloved figure in the culinary world, her journey has not been without obstacles. Like anyone pursuing ambitious goals, Ina faced moments of doubt, failure, and public criticism along the way. However, her ability to navigate these difficulties with grace and resilience has been key to her enduring success. Through setbacks, she found new opportunities, and in moments of self-doubt, she leaned on her support system, especially her husband, Jeffrey, to stay motivated.

Ina's challenges extended beyond her career. As her public profile grew, so did the pressures of fame, forcing her to strike a delicate balance between her work and personal life. Navigating the demands of television, cookbooks, product development, and media attention required careful planning and intentional boundary-setting. Ina chose to prioritize joy over perfection, declining projects that didn't align with her values to maintain a sense of balance and well-being. Her ability to focus on what matters most–her passions, relationships, and personal joy–has been essential in sustaining her career over the decades.

Ina's journey also highlights her thoughtful approach to handling public criticism and media attention. Rather than getting distracted by external noise, she has stayed true to her brand and personal philosophy, focusing on meaningful work that brings joy to her audience and herself.

This chapter explores the personal and professional challenges Ina has encountered throughout her career and the strategies she has used to overcome them. From setbacks and self-doubt to balancing a growing business with personal happiness, Ina's story offers valuable lessons on resilience, authenticity, and the importance of staying grounded. Her ability to thrive through challenges serves as a reminder that success is not about avoiding difficulties but about navigating them with intention, grace, and perseverance.

Overcoming Setbacks: Navigating Challenges and Finding Success

Throughout her career, Ina Garten has faced moments of uncertainty and challenges that pushed her beyond her comfort zone. One of the most significant periods of uncertainty came after she sold the Barefoot Contessa food store in East Hampton. Although the store had been a major success, Ina found herself at a crossroads, unsure of what the next chapter of her life would hold. She knew she didn't want to return to her previous government career, but she also wasn't certain what path to pursue. The decision to write her first cookbook was not made lightly–Ina had serious doubts about whether she could make the transition from business owner to author. Writing was unfamiliar territory, and she feared that her first attempt might fail. But with encouragement from Jeffrey and her close friends, she decided to take the risk, choosing to embrace the unknown.

The release of *The Barefoot Contessa Cookbook* in 1999 was a turning point, but the journey wasn't without challenges. As the media landscape evolved, Ina had to navigate changes in how audiences engaged with food content. While her cookbooks were initially successful, shifting consumer habits eventually required her to expand beyond traditional publishing. The growing popularity of television cooking shows presented a new opportunity, but it was also an unfamiliar challenge. Transitioning to television brought new pressures, as Ina had to learn how to present herself on camera while maintaining the same warmth and authenticity that defined her books. There were also moments when ideas didn't pan out or business ventures didn't align with her vision. Despite these setbacks, Ina remained focused, adapting her strategies to stay relevant in an ever-changing industry. Her persistence and willingness to learn kept her moving forward.

Self-doubt accompanied many of these transitions. When Ina first began filming *Barefoot Contessa* on the Food Network, she questioned whether she could translate her passion for cooking into a television format. Being in the public eye came with added pressure, and she had to manage the growing demands of her brand while staying true to herself. During these moments of uncertainty, Ina leaned heavily on her husband, Jeffrey, whose unwavering support gave her the confidence to push through. Jeffrey's belief in her abilities provided a steady foundation, reassuring Ina during moments when she questioned whether she was on the right path. She also relied on a close circle of trusted collaborators and friends who helped her stay grounded through challenging periods.

Ina's ability to overcome setbacks and uncertainty has been central to her enduring success. By embracing change, learning from failure, and leaning on her support system, she navigated challenges with grace. Her journey demonstrates that even the most accomplished individuals face obstacles–but it's persistence, adaptability, and support that ultimately lead to success.

Handling Criticism and Staying Grounded: Managing Media and Public Attention

As Ina Garten's public profile grew, so did the attention–both positive and critical–that came with being a high-profile figure. Although she is beloved by millions, even Ina hasn't been immune to public criticism and media scrutiny. Whether it involved personal decisions, professional choices, or public appearances, Ina has encountered moments when her actions were misunderstood or criticized. However, her ability to manage this attention with grace and poise has been a defining feature of her career.

One notable example occurred when Ina declined a request to participate in a Make-A-Wish event early in her television career, leading to public backlash. While the situation was later resolved, it highlighted the pressures public figures face when their personal boundaries are at odds with public expectations. Ina remained composed throughout the ordeal, focusing on her values and refusing to let external negativity derail her work. This ability to stay grounded, even in the face of criticism, has helped Ina maintain her focus on what matters most–creating meaningful content that brings joy to her audience.

Ina's strategy for handling criticism involves concentrating on her passion and staying true to herself. She avoids getting caught up in trends or public opinion, choosing instead to focus on her love for food and entertaining. By keeping her work aligned with her values and interests, she has built a brand that feels genuine and personal. This consistency has allowed Ina to weather moments of scrutiny without sacrificing her integrity. She focuses on her audience's trust and loyalty rather than the fleeting attention of critics.

Fame brings not only scrutiny but also intense pressure to meet expectations. Ina's ability to stay grounded in her work is a reflection of her personal philosophy: prioritize joy, simplicity, and authenticity. Rather than striving for perfection, Ina focuses on the pleasure of cooking and sharing food with others. Her authenticity resonates with audiences who see her as not just a celebrity but as someone they can relate to—a person who values meaningful experiences over public approval.

Maintaining privacy has also been essential to Ina's sense of balance. She sets clear boundaries between her public and personal lives, engaging with her fans on her own terms. Through social media, newsletters, and personal anecdotes, she offers glimpses into her world, but she is intentional about what she shares. This boundary-setting allows her to manage public attention while keeping the most important aspects of her life—her relationship with Jeffrey and her personal happiness—out of the spotlight.

Ina's approach to criticism and media attention serves as a model of resilience. By staying focused on her passions, setting boundaries, and embracing authenticity, she has maintained both her personal well-being and the integrity of her brand. Her ability to handle public scrutiny with grace ensures that her influence remains enduring and meaningful.

Finding Balance: Navigating the Intersection of Career and Personal Life

Throughout her career, Ina Garten has skillfully managed to strike a balance between professional success and personal fulfillment. As her brand grew to include bestselling cookbooks, a hit television show, and product collaborations, the demands on her time increased exponentially. Yet, despite her many professional commitments, Ina has always prioritized her personal life, ensuring that her relationship with Jeffrey and her sense of joy remain central to everything she does. Achieving this balance has required intentional decisions, thoughtful boundaries, and a commitment to focusing on what truly matters.

One of the ways Ina maintains balance is by carefully choosing which projects to take on. Rather than saying yes to every opportunity, she focuses only on those that align with her values and bring her joy. This intentional approach allows her to manage her workload while still having time for herself and her loved ones. By being selective, she prevents burnout and ensures that every project she undertakes is meaningful and enjoyable. Ina has often shared that she only pursues work that makes her happy—whether writing cookbooks, filming episodes of *Barefoot Contessa*, or developing new recipes.

Creating routines and rituals has also helped Ina stay grounded. She and Jeffrey maintain daily habits that strengthen their relationship, such as phone calls when Jeffrey is traveling and quiet weekend dinners at their East Hampton home. These small moments of connection offer a sense of stability amid Ina's busy schedule. Their relationship provides her with the support and joy needed to navigate the challenges of a demanding career.

In addition to her personal routines, Ina carves out time for relaxation and enjoyment, balancing her love for work with moments of rest. She values the quiet life she shares with Jeffrey in East Hampton, where she enjoys gardening, taking long walks, and hosting friends. These everyday activities help her recharge and remain connected to the things that bring her peace and fulfillment.

Setting boundaries has been another crucial factor in Ina's ability to find balance. She knows the importance of saying no to projects that don't align with her goals or would overwhelm her schedule. This boundary-setting allows her to focus on what brings her the most joy and ensures that she has time for her personal life. Ina's selective approach to fame—avoiding overexposure in the media and engaging with fans on her own terms—also helps her maintain a sense of control over her public presence.

Ina's story demonstrates that success and personal fulfillment are not mutually exclusive. Through thoughtful decisions, daily rituals, and clear boundaries, she has created a life that balances career growth with personal happiness. Her ability to stay grounded amid professional demands serves as a model for others, showing that it's possible to pursue ambitious goals while nurturing the relationships and routines that make life meaningful.

Leaning on Support Systems: The Role of Relationships in Navigating Challenges

Ina Garten's success is not the product of individual effort alone–it is deeply intertwined with the support she receives from those closest to her. At the center of that support system is her husband, Jeffrey, whose unwavering belief in her has been a constant source of encouragement throughout her career. During moments of uncertainty or doubt, Jeffrey's steady presence gave Ina the confidence to pursue bold new ventures, from writing her first cookbook to stepping in front of the camera for *Barefoot Contessa*. His optimism and love have not only supported her career growth but have also provided emotional stability during stressful times.

Beyond her relationship with Jeffrey, Ina has cultivated a close circle of friends, collaborators, and colleagues who play essential roles in both her personal life and professional endeavors. Many of her most trusted collaborators have worked with her for years, helping her test recipes, develop cookbooks, and manage her television projects. Their shared values–attention to detail, authenticity, and simplicity–create an environment of mutual respect and trust, making every project a joyful experience rather than a stressful task.

Ina's friendships within the culinary and media worlds have also contributed to her resilience. By surrounding herself with individuals who share her passion for food, entertaining, and meaningful work, she has built a community that nurtures her creativity. These relationships offer support, advice, and encouragement during challenging moments. Whether it's brainstorming new ideas or simply sharing a meal together, Ina's friendships are a vital source of inspiration and joy.

Maintaining these personal connections has been a priority for Ina, even as her career demands grew. She and Jeffrey are known for hosting intimate gatherings with friends at their East Hampton home, creating opportunities to connect with loved ones away from the public eye. These gatherings reflect her belief that relationships are strengthened not through grand gestures but through shared moments of joy and hospitality.

Ina's ability to lean on her support system—whether through the love of her husband, the loyalty of collaborators, or the companionship of friends—has been crucial to her success. These relationships provide the emotional and practical support necessary to navigate the pressures of public life and the demands of running a business. They remind her of what truly matters: meaningful connections, shared experiences, and the joy of creating together. Ina's story demonstrates the importance of building and nurturing relationships that uplift and inspire, offering a valuable lesson in the power of community and support.

Triumph Through Resilience: Lessons from Challenges and Success

Ina Garten's journey is one defined by resilience—her ability to navigate setbacks, embrace change, and grow through challenges has been a key factor in her enduring success. From the uncertainty of leaving government work to the challenges of writing her first cookbook, every obstacle Ina encountered became an opportunity for growth. Her story offers valuable lessons in perseverance, adaptability, and the importance of maintaining a positive outlook, even in the face of difficulties.

One of the essential lessons Ina has learned is that failure is not the end but part of the process. Early in her career, she faced doubts about whether she could make a successful transition from running a food store to becoming an author and television personality. There were moments when she questioned her abilities, but rather than seeing these doubts as roadblocks, Ina treated them as part of the journey.

Every mistake or challenge became an opportunity to learn, improve, and move forward.

Resilience also meant staying true to her values, even when external pressures suggested otherwise. In an industry that often favors rapid growth and trend-chasing, Ina remained focused on meaningful work. She resisted the temptation to overextend her brand, choosing instead to pursue projects that aligned with her passion for food, entertaining, and authentic living. Her ability to stay selective and intentional has been a cornerstone of her long-term success.

Another key aspect of Ina's resilience is her gratitude and appreciation for life's small joys. She focuses on what brings her happiness–whether it's a simple meal with Jeffrey, time spent in her garden, or a weekend cooking with friends. This mindset helps Ina maintain perspective, reminding her that success is not just about achievements but also about savoring everyday moments.

Ina's journey offers a powerful example of how to navigate the intersection of personal happiness and professional success. Through persistence, intentional choices, and a focus on joy, she has built a life and career that reflect her values. Her ability to triumph through challenges serves as an inspiration to others, showing that resilience is not about avoiding obstacles but about finding the strength to embrace them. As Ina's story demonstrates, the path to success is rarely linear–but with passion, patience, and the right support, every challenge can become an opportunity for growth.

Ina Garten's journey has been shaped by resilience, thoughtful choices, and the support of those closest to her. Through setbacks, public scrutiny, and moments of self-doubt, she has stayed true to her values, embracing challenges as opportunities for growth. Her ability to balance personal happiness with professional success offers a powerful example of how to navigate life's complexities with grace. By prioritizing meaningful work, nurturing relationships, and savoring small joys, Ina has built a life that reflects her passions. Her story reminds us that success isn't about avoiding obstacles but about thriving through them with patience, authenticity, and perseverance.

CHAPTER 10

LOOKING FORWARD: THE FUTURE OF INA GARTEN

Ina Garten's career has been nothing short of extraordinary, but her journey is far from over. With decades of experience, bestselling cookbooks, a beloved television show, and an enduring lifestyle brand, Ina has cemented herself as a culinary icon. Yet, as the food world continues to evolve, so does Ina's role within it. In this chapter, we explore what lies ahead for Ina, reflecting on her legacy, her thoughts on the future of food, and the projects she still hopes to pursue. Ina's influence extends beyond recipes–her philosophy of joyful cooking and entertaining has redefined how we think about food, hospitality, and living well.

As the culinary landscape shifts toward sustainability, plant-based eating, and digital engagement, Ina has already begun to adapt. While her core philosophy remains rooted in simplicity, her curiosity about emerging food trends suggests that she will continue evolving with the times. Ina's ability to stay relevant through thoughtful, meaningful growth has ensured that her brand feels timeless, even as trends come and go.

Looking forward, we'll consider the new ventures Ina may explore and how she plans to maintain her influence in the years to come. Whether through new cookbooks, creative collaborations, or expanded product lines, Ina's journey continues with the same authenticity and intentionality that have defined her career.

Ina has also become a mentor to aspiring cooks, chefs, and entrepreneurs, inspiring them to pursue work that aligns with their passions. In this chapter, we'll explore the advice she offers to those looking to follow in her footsteps, encouraging them to embrace joy, authenticity, and quality in everything they do. As Ina continues her journey, one thing is certain: her legacy will inspire and shape the culinary world for generations to come.

A Lifetime of Culinary Influence: Redefining Home Cooking

Ina Garten's legacy extends beyond recipes–she has transformed the way people cook and entertain at home, leaving a lasting impact on the culinary world. Her focus on simplicity, quality ingredients, and joyful cooking has shaped modern home cooking in profound ways. From her debut cookbook to her long-running television show, Ina has made the kitchen a place of pleasure rather than stress, empowering home cooks to feel confident in preparing delicious meals without complex techniques. She has redefined what it means to cook at home, demonstrating that great food can be accessible, elegant, and deeply enjoyable.

One of Ina's most significant contributions is her philosophy of simplicity. At a time when many chefs emphasize intricate recipes and restaurant-style plating, Ina has always promoted cooking with a handful of high-quality ingredients. She believes that fresh, seasonal produce, good olive oil, and artisanal bread can elevate even the simplest meals. Her recipes reflect this ethos, featuring dishes like roast chicken, baked salmon, and simple pastas that celebrate natural flavors. By stripping away unnecessary complexity, Ina encourages home cooks to focus on what really matters: enjoying food with loved ones.

Ina's influence extends beyond the kitchen to the way people entertain. She has revolutionized the concept of hospitality by promoting relaxed, effortless entertaining. Rather than elaborate dinner parties with complicated menus, Ina teaches her audience to focus on creating warm, welcoming gatherings. She emphasizes that the joy of entertaining lies in connection, not perfection, and her make-ahead strategies and easy appetizers have become staples for those looking to host without stress. This shift from formal hosting to casual, meaningful gatherings has resonated deeply with modern audiences, inspiring a new way of thinking about hospitality.

Ina's global reach is another hallmark of her influence. Although she started her career with a small food store in East Hampton, her impact has grown far beyond the Hamptons. Through her cookbooks, television show, and online presence, Ina has built a community of home cooks who trust her guidance. Her fans appreciate not only her foolproof recipes but also the glimpses into her life with Jeffrey, which add a personal touch to her brand. The authenticity and warmth she exudes have made her a trusted figure in kitchens worldwide.

In addition to changing the way people cook and entertain, Ina has set new standards for reliability in food media. Her meticulous recipe testing ensures that every dish works perfectly, building trust with readers and viewers. This focus on quality and consistency has earned her a reputation as one of the most dependable voices in the culinary world. Home cooks know that when they open an Ina Garten cookbook or watch an episode of *Barefoot Contessa*, they will find approachable, reliable recipes that deliver excellent results every time.

Ultimately, Ina's influence goes beyond individual recipes–it lies in the way she has reshaped attitudes toward food and hospitality. She has shown that cooking can be a source of joy and that entertaining should be about making people feel welcome, not about impressing them. Ina's philosophy of simplicity, quality, and connection has created a lasting legacy, inspiring home cooks to approach the kitchen with confidence and delight. As her career continues to evolve, her impact on home cooking and entertaining will endure, influencing generations to come.

The Evolving Food Landscape: Ina's Perspective on the Future

The culinary world is constantly evolving, and Ina Garten has demonstrated her ability to adapt to new trends while remaining true to her core philosophy. As the food landscape shifts toward sustainability, plant-based eating, and digital media, Ina continues to embrace these changes thoughtfully, integrating them into her work without compromising her values. Her perspective on the future of food reflects both her experience and her open-mindedness, making her an enduring figure in an industry known for rapid change.

One of the most significant shifts in the culinary world today is the increasing focus on sustainability. As consumers become more mindful of where their food comes from, there is a growing demand for local, seasonal ingredients and reduced food waste. Ina has long been an advocate of using fresh, high-quality ingredients, often highlighting the importance of buying locally whenever possible. Her recipes reflect a seasonal approach to cooking, encouraging home cooks to use what is freshest and most available. This alignment with sustainable practices positions Ina as a voice of relevance in a food culture that is becoming increasingly eco-conscious.

Plant-based eating is another trend that has gained significant momentum in recent years, and Ina has shown a willingness to embrace it. While her signature dishes often feature meat, she has expanded her repertoire to include more plant-forward recipes, such as vibrant vegetable salads and hearty soups. This openness to evolving dietary preferences demonstrates Ina's adaptability and her commitment to staying relevant in a changing culinary landscape. Though she remains true to her love of indulgent comfort food, she acknowledges the importance of variety and balance in modern cooking.

The rise of digital media and technology has also transformed the way people engage with food content. Social media platforms, virtual cooking classes, and online communities now play a significant role in how audiences connect with chefs and cooking experts. While Ina's brand was built through traditional cookbooks and television, she has embraced the digital shift in her own way. Her social media presence offers fans glimpses into her personal life, as well as cooking inspiration and entertaining ideas. Ina's ability to engage with her audience through Instagram and newsletters demonstrates her understanding of the importance of staying connected in an increasingly digital world.

Looking ahead, Ina is likely to continue evolving with the times while staying rooted in her core philosophy. Whether through future collaborations, online projects, or expanded product lines, she remains open to exploring new opportunities that align with her values. However, her cautious approach to fame and media ensures that any new venture will reflect the authenticity that defines her brand. Rather than chasing trends, Ina carefully integrates modern elements into her work, ensuring her relevance while maintaining her identity.

Ina Garten's perspective on the future of food is a blend of tradition and innovation. She embraces change without abandoning her guiding principles of simplicity, quality, and joy. As the culinary world continues to evolve, Ina's influence will remain strong, not only for the recipes she creates but for the thoughtful, intentional way she approaches both food and life.

Continuing the Journey: What Lies Ahead for Ina Garten

As Ina Garten reflects on her decades of success, she shows no signs of slowing down. Although she has built a remarkable career spanning bestselling cookbooks, a hit television series, product collaborations, and a devoted fanbase, Ina's journey is far from over. She continues to pursue meaningful projects that align with her passions and values. Her ability to evolve thoughtfully while staying true to her core philosophy of simplicity, quality, and joy suggests that exciting opportunities lie ahead in both her professional and personal life.

Future cookbooks remain a likely part of Ina's journey. Her fans eagerly await every new release, knowing each will bring fresh inspiration while maintaining the approachable style they have come to love. With her focus on current culinary trends, future books could explore themes like plant-based meals, holiday entertaining, or health-conscious comfort food. Another possibility is a memoir-style cookbook, blending new recipes with stories from her life, offering fans deeper insight into her experiences. Given her enduring curiosity, it's easy to imagine that Ina has many more culinary ideas waiting to be shared.

In addition to cookbooks, there are other potential avenues for Ina's creative energy. Online projects, such as virtual cooking classes or digital courses, could allow her to reach new audiences while expanding her brand. The rise of digital engagement, especially after the pandemic, has opened doors for chefs and entertainers to connect with fans through virtual platforms. Ina's warm, approachable style would translate well to these formats, offering people the opportunity to learn from her in real time.

Product collaborations may also remain part of her future. Given her passion for home cooking and entertaining, she could expand her offerings beyond cookware and food products to include lifestyle items like linens, home décor, or entertaining essentials. These additions would align with her brand's focus on creating meaningful experiences at home. With her emphasis on quality, any new product venture would reflect the same care and attention to detail that define her recipes and shows.

However, even as she pursues new opportunities, Ina will likely remain selective. Her cautious approach to fame has served her well, allowing her to grow her brand while maintaining balance and authenticity. She continues to focus on meaningful work rather than chasing trends or engaging in overexposure. This intentionality ensures that every project she takes on resonates with her audience and stays true to her identity.

On a personal level, Ina also looks forward to continuing the life she has built with Jeffrey. Their relationship, which has been a constant source of joy and stability throughout her career, remains at the heart of everything she does. Ina often mentions how much she enjoys their quiet moments at home, from sharing dinners to spending weekends together in the garden. These personal experiences not only recharge her but also inspire many of the ideas she shares in her cookbooks and on her show.

As she navigates the next chapter of her journey, Ina's focus will likely remain on doing what she loves while bringing joy to others. Whether through future cookbooks, new ventures, or personal projects, Ina shows that success is not just about achievements but about continuing to find fulfillment in meaningful work. With her signature warmth and authenticity, Ina Garten's journey is far from over–it continues to evolve with joy, purpose, and grace.

Advice for Aspiring Cooks and Entrepreneurs: Ina's Words of Wisdom

Over the years, Ina Garten has become not just a culinary icon but also a source of inspiration for aspiring cooks, chefs, and entrepreneurs. Through her books, television show, and interviews, she offers valuable advice for those hoping to pursue careers in food or build successful businesses. Ina's words of wisdom reflect her belief that success comes from passion, authenticity, and a thoughtful approach to growth–principles that have guided her throughout her own journey.

One of Ina's key pieces of advice is to follow your passion. She often emphasizes the importance of doing work that brings joy, noting that her own success stemmed from taking risks to pursue what she loved. Leaving her government career to open the Barefoot Contessa store was a leap of faith, but it allowed her to build a life she found fulfilling. Ina encourages aspiring entrepreneurs to take similar risks, even if the path ahead feels uncertain. According to her, loving what you do makes all the difference–success becomes more meaningful when it's rooted in passion.

In addition to following your passion, Ina stresses the importance of simplicity and quality. Whether in cooking or business, she believes that less is often more. For home cooks, this means using a few excellent ingredients to create flavorful dishes rather than complicating things with elaborate techniques. For entrepreneurs, it means focusing on thoughtful growth instead of chasing trends. Ina's emphasis on quality over quantity reminds aspiring chefs and business owners that building trust with your audience is essential. Offering something authentic and reliable, she says, will always resonate more deeply than following the latest fad.

Another lesson from Ina is the importance of authenticity. She has built her career by staying true to herself, avoiding overexposure, and pursuing projects that align with her values. She advises others to do the same–whether starting a business, writing a cookbook, or building a personal brand. Authenticity not only fosters trust but also makes the journey more enjoyable. Ina's story is a testament to the fact that staying true to your identity, even in a fast-changing world, leads to lasting success.

For aspiring entrepreneurs, Ina also emphasizes the value of patience and intentionality. She advises people not to rush into every opportunity but to choose projects carefully and focus on what matters most. Her career is proof that slow, thoughtful growth is more sustainable than rapid expansion. Ina believes that it's okay to say no to opportunities that don't feel right–doing so ensures that your work remains meaningful and aligned with your vision.

Finally, Ina offers a reminder to enjoy the process. She encourages home cooks to have fun in the kitchen and not to worry about perfection. For entrepreneurs, she advises embracing the ups and downs of building a business, recognizing that mistakes are part of the journey. Ina believes that the ultimate goal is not just success but creating a life you love–a life filled with joy, meaningful relationships, and personal fulfillment.

Ina Garten's advice reflects the wisdom she has gained from decades of experience. Whether in cooking, business, or life, her message is clear: Follow your passion, stay true to yourself, and focus on what brings joy. Her words inspire aspiring cooks and entrepreneurs to approach their journeys with thoughtfulness, patience, and authenticity, knowing that success lies not just in the outcome but in the joy of the process itself.

CONCLUSION

Ina Garten's journey is a testament to the power of passion, authenticity, and thoughtful growth. As she reflects on her accomplishments, it's clear that her legacy goes beyond cookbooks and television–it lies in the way she has redefined home cooking and hospitality. With a focus on simplicity, quality, and connection, Ina has inspired millions to embrace the joy of cooking and create meaningful moments with loved ones.

As the culinary landscape continues to evolve, Ina's ability to adapt while staying true to her values ensures that her influence will endure. Whether she pursues new cookbooks, expands her lifestyle brand, or engages with her audience through digital platforms, she will continue to bring joy to those who follow her work.

Ina's advice to aspiring cooks and entrepreneurs–pursue what you love, stay authentic, and focus on quality–offers timeless wisdom for anyone looking to build a fulfilling life or career. Her journey is far from over, and whatever lies ahead, she will undoubtedly continue to inspire others with her grace, warmth, and passion. As Ina looks to the future, she reminds us that success is not just about achievements–it's about finding joy in the process and living a life filled with meaning.